THE REALLY

CHRISTMAS Cook Book

CATHY BRIDGES

MEREHURST

Published in 1995 by Merehurst Limited
Ferry House, 51-57 Lacy Road, Putney, London SW15 1PR

ISBN 1-85391-454-1

A catalogue record for this book is available from the British Library

Series Editor: Valerie Barrett
Design: Clive Dorman
Illustrations: Keith Sparrow

Typeset by Clive Dorman & Co.
Colour Separation by P&W Graphics Pty Ltd, Singapore
Printed and bound in Great Britain by
Mackays of Chatham PLC

RECIPE NOTES

- 35 Indicates dishes that cook in under 35 minutes
- Follow one set of measurements only, do not mix metric and imperial
- All spoon measures are level
- Always taste and adjust seasonings to suit your own preferences
- V Indicates dishes that are suitable for vegetarians

CONTENTS

Introduction 4

Reference guide to:
preparing, cooking and storing
Christmas poultry, meat and perishables 5

Savouries and Drinks 12

Starters 25

Main Course Dishes 39

Sauces, Stuffings and Accompaniments 57

Vegetables 67

Salads 80

Desserts 96

Cakes 112

Tea Time Treats 130

Dishes with Leftovers 143

Index 159

INTRODUCTION

Christmas is a time for celebration and that includes lots of festive eating and drinking. It can be difficult trying to organise large family meals and parties for friends amidst all the other chaos of putting up decorations, present buying and wrapping and so on. It is best to plan your meals in advance and with the help of the large selection of recipes in this book you should be able to find something to suit everyone.

There are many ideas from old favourites and variations to interesting new alternatives. The recipes range from savoury nibbles and starters through to desserts, tea time treats and dishes to use up the leftovers. There are plenty of main course and side dishes suitable for vegetarians and many new suggestions for those who want to break away from very traditional food.

For many people the biggest problem is how to deal with The Turkey. The Reference Guide will inform you on every aspect of this special Christmas food – what size to choose, how to thaw, stuff, truss, cook and carve it.

Use this book to help you plan your Christmas meals and when ideas run thin or last minute panic sets in, keep it to hand for inspiration and guidance.

Merry Christmas!

REFERENCE GUIDE TO:
PREPARING, COOKING AND STORING CHRISTMAS POULTRY, MEAT AND PERISHABLES

GUIDE TO THAWING TURKEY AND CHICKEN

Frozen turkey and chicken must be thoroughly thawed before cooking to avoid the risk of salmonella food poisoning. Allow the bird to thaw in its bag in a cool place, preferably below 15°C (60°F) using the chart below as a guide. Remember the lower the room temperature the longer it will take to thaw. If you thaw the turkey in the fridge allow extra time. NEVER thaw a bird in hot water. When thawed, the legs will be flexible and there will be no trace of ice crystals in the body cavity. Wash the inside of the turkey or chicken thoroughly under cold running water and then pat dry with kitchen paper.

THAWING AND SERVING CHART

Oven-Ready Weight	No. of Servings	Thawing time *
1.5-2.5 kg (3-5 lb)	4-6	20 hours
3-3.5 kg (6-7 lb)	7-9	30 hours
4-4.5 kg (8-9 lb)	10-14	36 hours
5-5.5 kg (10-11 lb)	15-16	45 hours
6-6.5 kg (12-13 lb)	17-18	48 hours
7-8.5 kg (14-17 lb)	19-25	48 hours
9-11 kg (18-22 lb)	26-35	48 hours
13 kg (23 lb) plus	35 plus	48 hours

* Times based on thawing at 15°C (60°F)

STUFFING THE BIRD

Before stuffing the turkey or chicken, make sure that the stuffing is completely cold. Only stuff the neck cavity of the bird to ensure the heat penetrates the centre and cooks the meat quickly and thoroughly. Take care not to pack the stuffing too tightly or the skin may split during cooking. Any extra stuffing may be shaped into balls and placed in an ovenproof dish and cooked separately. A cut apple and peeled onion placed inside the body cavity also adds extra flavour. The stuffing may be prepared a day in advance and kept covered in the refrigerator until needed. Allow about 250g (8 oz) prepared stuffing per 2.5 kg (5 lb) dressed weight of turkey.

TRUSSING THE BIRD

After the bird has been stuffed, it should be trussed in order to help it retain a good shape whilst cooking.

1 Place the bird breast side down. Pull the loose neck skin over the neck cavity and tuck the wing tips under. Secure the neck skin with a metal skewer, securing the wing tips to the body at the same time.

2 To secure the upper drumsticks, turn the bird breast side up. Thread a trussing needle with fine string and pass it through the upper part of one drumstick, then the body and through the other drumstick. Remove the needle and pull the string so a length of string is protruding from both drumsticks.

3 To secure the lower drumsticks, turn the bird over and cross the string over its back. Turn the bird again so it is once more breast-side up. Cross the ends of the string and tie drumsticks and 'parson's nose' together with a secure knot.

4 Place the bird breast-side up in a roasting pan ready to cook.

ROASTING THE TURKEY

When calculating the cooking time, always use the oven-ready weight, i.e. the bird after stuffing. Time the cooking for the bird to be ready 15 minutes before carving as the resting time helps ensure that the flesh firms up and this makes carving easier.

Place the bird in a roasting pan, and unless self-basting, brush the surface with melted butter. The breast may also be covered with bacon rashers to help keep the flesh moist. Alternatively, the turkey may be wrapped in foil or butter-soaked muslin. This reduces the need for basting during cooking.

Roast the bird at 190C,375F, Gas 5 according to the chart below. To test that the bird is cooked, pierce the thickest part of both thighs with a metal skewer. When cooked, the juices should run clear with no trace of pink.

Remove the bacon, foil or muslin 30 minutes before the end of the cooking time to allow the skin to become crisp and golden.

ROASTING CHART

Times based on roasting at 190C,375F, Gas 5.

Oven-Ready Weight	Without Foil	Wrapped in Foil
1.5-2.5 kg (3-5 lb)	1½-1¾ hours	1¾-2 hours
3-3.5 kg (6-7 lb)	1¾-2 hours	2-2¼ hours
4-4.5 kg (8-9 lb)	2-2½ hours	2½-2¾ hours
5-5.5 kg (10-11 lb)	2/4-2¾ hours	2½-3 hours
6-6.5 kg (12-13 lb)	2¾-3 hours	3-3¼ hours
7-8.5 kg (14-17 lb)	3¼-3½ hours	3½-3¾ hours
9-11 kg (18-22 lb)	3½ -3¾ hours	3¾-4 hours
13 kg (23 lb) plus	3¾ hours plus	4½ hours plus

CARVING THE TURKEY

1 Use a pointed knife with a very sharp edge and a long, flexible blade. To remove the first leg remove the string and skewers and place the bird breast-side up on a carving board or plate. Hold the bird steady with a large carving fork. Cut the skin between the thigh and breast. Separate the leg from the body of the turkey by bending the thigh outwards to locate the hip joint, slice down through the joint to remove the leg.

2 To separate the thigh from the drumstick hold the knife at an angle between the thigh and drumstick bones and cut firmly through the joint to separate the leg into two serving portions.

3 To slice the drumstick cut thick slices of meat from each side of the bone, keeping the knife close to the bone. Cut these into smaller slices.

4 To slice the thigh, hold steady with a fork and slice into 4 or more pieces depending on the size of the thigh. Repeat steps 1-4 on the other side of the turkey.

5 To remove the wing, slice down through the corner of the breast towards the wing. Push the wing out to show the joint and cut through the joint. Remove the wing with a piece of breast attached.

6 To carve the breast, hold steady with a carving fork and slice down through the meat. When one side is carved, remove the other wing and carve the remaining breast meat.

STORING AND REHEATING LEFTOVER TURKEY OR CHICKEN

Leftover cooked poultry should be cooled, covered and refrigerated as soon as possible after cooking. Leftover stuffing should be removed from the bird and stored in a separate dish in the fridge. Cooked turkey or chicken should be eaten within 2 days or it can be frozen for up to 2 months. Drumsticks, wings and thighs can be frozen on the bone, or the meat can be diced or sliced for convenience ready to add a sauce for reheating. Wrap the cold turkey or chicken meat in foil or freezer wrap and label and freeze. Allow to thaw thoroughly before reheating. When reheating cooked turkey or chicken meat, make sure it boils for at least 5 minutes and that the meat is piping hot all the way through. Do not reheat cooked turkey or chicken more than once, or refreeze it.

HOW TO MAKE TURKEY STOCK

A good flavoursome turkey stock makes an excellent base for soups and casseroles and can be used in recipes for leftover turkey.

To make the stock, put the turkey carcass and bones into a large saucepan. Add 1 sliced onion, a sprig of fresh thyme or bouquet garni, 2 sticks chopped celery and 4 whole cloves. Cover with cold water, bring to the boil, then simmer for 1½ hours. Allow to cool and then strain and skim off any fat.

Ideally stock should be made and used on the same day, but it can be cooled and stored in the fridge for up to 2 days. Stock may also be frozen for up to 2 months. Boil the prepared stock over a high heat to reduce by half. Cool and then pour into ice cube trays and freeze until solid. Transfer to plastic freezer bags and label. Alternatively pour into suitable containers allowing about 2.5 cm (1 inch) headroom as the stock expands on freezing.

To use frozen stock cubes, thaw at room temperature or simply add to a saucepan and heat gently, stirring occasionally. Add 1 tablespoon water to each concentrated stock cube.

HOW TO COOK GAMMON AND BACON

Bacon and gammon joints are traditionally served as part of a cold meat platter at Christmas. Always check when purchasing the joint whether it needs soaking before cooking, to remove excess saltiness. When advised to soak the joint, place in a saucepan of cold water and bring to the boil. Drain the water and cover with fresh water ready for cooking. Bring the water to the boil, then reduce heat and simmer for 20 minutes per 500g (1 lb), plus an extra 20 minutes, keeping the pan topped up with boiling water. For cooked joints which are to be glazed and baked, allow 10 minutes boiling time per 500g (1 lb), plus 10 minutes extra, then bake in an oven preheated to 220°C,425°F, Gas 7 for 10 minutes per 500g (1 lb), plus an extra 10 minutes. For joints over 5 kg (10 lb) allow 20 minutes cooking time per 500g (1 lb).

HOW TO STORE PERISHABLE FOODS

Meat and fresh poultry

Remove all packaging. Cover loosely with greaseproof paper and place in the meat compartment or the coldest part of the fridge, away from cooked foods or dairy produce such as milk or cheese. Place on a tray or plate so that nothing can drip on to food underneath.

Fresh fish

Place scaled and cleaned fish in an airtight container and keep only for 1-2 days. Fish may be stored for longer in the freezer.

Soft fruits (except bananas) and salad vegetables

Store in the salad compartment in the fridge. Melons, strawberries and pineapple should be placed in sealed containers to prevent their flavours penetrating other foods.

Milk and cream

Wipe containers before placing in the fridge. Follow packaging instructions regarding storage times.

Cheese

Wrap loosely in greaseproof paper or foil and store in the fridge.

Eggs

Store in the carton in the fridge.

Bread

Leave in plastic wrapper or store in a bread bin which must be cleaned and aired regularly. Bread may also be stored in the freezer and slices taken out as needed. Never keep bread in the fridge.

Onions and potatoes

Store in a cool dark, well-ventilated place.

Root vegetables, pears, apples etc

Keep in the fridge or a cool, dark place.

Cakes and biscuits

Store separately in clean, airtight containers.

SAVOURIES AND DRINKS

Christmas is a time for entertaining and it is nice to be able to greet friends with a celebratory drink and something tasty to nibble. Here are some easy to prepare ideas that will put everyone in the festive spirit.

35

PRAWNS WITH CREAMY PESTO

REALLY EASY!

This dish can be prepared several hours in advance and stored, covered, in the refrigerator until required. Ready-made pesto is available from Italian delicatessens and some supermarkets.

Serves 6-8

1 kg (2 lb) cooked medium prawns, shelled and deveined, tails left intact
2 carrots, cut into thick strips
200g (7 oz) mangetout, blanched
1 red pepper, seeded and cut into thick strips

Creamy Pesto Dip

125g (4 oz) ready-made pesto
125 ml (4 fl oz) thick mayonnaise

1 To make the dip, place pesto and mayonnaise in a bowl and mix to combine.

2 To serve, place dip in a small bowl on a large serving platter and surround with prawns, carrots, mangetout and red pepper.

35

V

CRUDITÉS WITH GARLIC DIP

REALLY EASY!

Colourful crunchy vegetables with a garlic mayonnaise dip.

Serves 4-6

2 red or yellow peppers
12 radishes
12 baby carrots
½ cucumber
125g (4 oz) small mangetout
12 baby corn
2 sticks of celery
12 quail's eggs, optional
fresh herb sprigs to garnish

Garlic Dip

8 tablespoons thick mayonnaise
2-3 cloves garlic, crushed
salt and pepper to taste

1 To make the dip, mix the mayonnaise with garlic, salt and pepper in a bowl.

2 Halve and seed the peppers and cut into long wedges. Trim the radishes, leaving on a little greenery at the ends. Peel and trim the carrots. Halve the cucumber lengthwise, scoop out the seeds and cut into sticks. Blanch mangetout and baby corn in boiling water for 1 minute: refresh in cold water and drain. Trim celery and cut into sticks.

3 If used, place the quail's eggs in a saucepan of cold water to cover and bring to the boil. Boil for 2 minutes, then plunge the eggs into cold water to cool. Partially peel the eggs.

4 Arrange the vegetables and eggs on a large platter or individual serving plates. Cover and chill until required. Garnish with herb sprigs and serve with garlic dip.

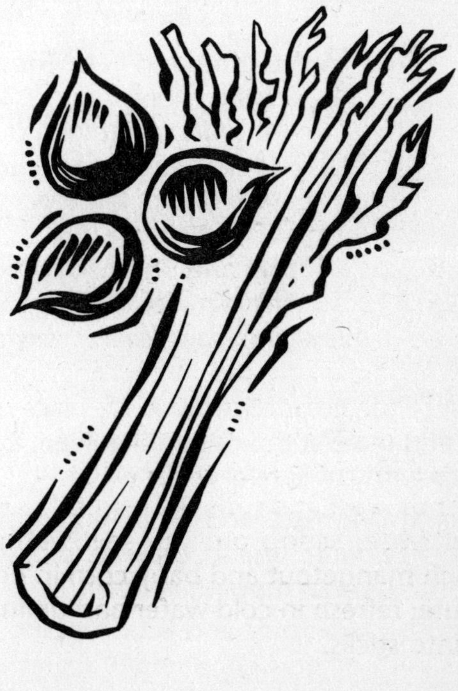

35

BRUSCHETTA

REALLY EASY!

V

Crunchy garlic toasts with 3 different toppings.

Makes 16-20

1 large French bread stick, cut into 1 cm (½ inch) slices
olive oil for brushing
2 cloves garlic, halved

Tomato and Basil Topping

2 tomatoes, sliced
1 red onion, sliced
2 tablespoons shredded fresh basil leaves

Aubergine and Feta Topping

2 baby aubergines, sliced
1 tablespoon olive oil
125g (4 oz) feta cheese, crumbled
freshly ground black pepper

Brie and Sage Topping

180g (6 oz) Brie, sliced
a few fresh sage leaves, roughly torn

1 Brush the bread slices with oil, place under a preheated grill and toast both sides until golden. Rub one side of the toasts with cut side of garlic cloves.

2 For the Tomato and Basil Topping, top some of the toast slices with tomato, onion and basil, and grill for 1-2 minutes or until topping is warm.

3 For the Aubergine and Feta Topping, brush aubergine slices with oil and cook under a preheated grill for 3-4 minutes each side or until lightly browned. Top the toasts with aubergine slices and sprinkle with feta cheese and black pepper to taste. Cook under a preheated grill for 1-

2 minutes or until topping is warm.

4 For Brie and Sage Topping arrange slices of Brie and sage leaves on the toasts. Place under a preheated grill and cook for 1-2 minutes or until cheese just melts.

MINI SPINACH TARTS

EASY!

The pastry cases can be made up to 3 days in advance and stored in an airtight container. Or make the cases several weeks in advance and freeze them. The filling mixture can be made earlier in the day, then covered and kept in the refrigerator until just prior to cooking.

Makes 20

Pastry

180g (6 oz) plain flour
4 tablespoons freshly grated Parmesan cheese
100g (3½ oz) butter, chopped
2-3 tablespoons iced water

Spinach Filling

2 teaspoons olive oil
2 spring onions, chopped
1 clove garlic, crushed
8 spinach leaves, shredded
125g (4 oz) ricotta cheese, drained
2 eggs, lightly beaten
90 ml (3 fl oz) milk
½ teaspoon grated nutmeg
4 tablespoons pine nuts

1 To make the pastry, put the flour, Parmesan cheese and butter into a food processor and process until mixture resembles fine breadcrumbs. (Or rub the mixture in with the fingertips until it resembles fine breadcrumbs.)

2 With machine running, slowly add enough water to form a soft dough. Turn dough onto a lightly floured surface and knead briefly. Wrap dough in plastic food wrap and refrigerate for 30 minutes.

3 Preheat the oven to 200C,400F, Gas 6.Roll out the pastry to 3 mm (⅛ inch) thick. Using an 8 cm (3½ inch) fluted pastry cutter, cut out 20 pastry rounds. Place pastry rounds in lightly greased patty tins. Prick base and sides of pastry with a fork and bake in the oven for 5-10 minutes or until lightly golden.

4 To make the filling, heat the oil in a frying pan over a medium heat. Add spring onions, garlic and spinach and cook, stirring, until spinach is wilted. Remove pan from heat and set aside to cool.

5 Place spinach mixture, ricotta cheese, eggs, milk and nutmeg in a bowl and mix to combine. Spoon filling into pastry cases and sprinkle with pine nuts. Reduce oven temperature to 180C,350F, Gas 4 and bake for 15-20 minutes or until tarts are golden and filling is set.

35

V

STILTON GRAPES

REALLY EASY!

To serve these delicious morsels you might like to arrange them in the shape of a bunch of grapes. If you have either a real or ornamental grape vine, use some of the leaves to decorate the plate.

Makes 30

125g (4 oz) cream cheese, softened
60g (2 oz) Stilton cheese, crumbled
2 tablespoons sour cream
30 large seedless green grapes
125g (4 oz) chopped shelled pistachio nuts

1 Place cream cheese, Stilton and sour cream in a bowl and beat until smooth.

2 Wrap each grape in a little cream cheese mixture then roll in pistachio nuts to coat. Refrigerate until firm.

35

V

RED BEAN DIP

REALLY EASY!

This recipe can also be made using dried red kidney beans but they will need to be soaked and cooked first. After soaking the water should be discarded and fresh water added for cooking. When cooking red kidney beans they must be boiled for 10 minutes first, to remove the toxins in the beans. The heat is then reduced to a simmer and the beans are cooked for 1¼-1½ hours or until tender.

2 tablespoons vegetable oil
1 clove garlic, crushed
1 onion, chopped
1 fresh green chilli, seeded and finely chopped
1 teaspoon chilli powder
400g (14 oz) can red kidney beans, drained and liquid reserved
60g (2 oz) mature Cheddar, finely grated
tortilla chips to serve

1 Heat the oil in a large frying pan, add garlic, onion, chilli and chilli powder and cook over a medium heat, stirring, for 4 minutes or until onion is soft.

2 Place all but 3 tablespoons of the beans in a food processor or blender and process until smooth. Add bean purée and 2 tablespoons reserved liquid to pan and mix well to combine.

3 Stir in the cheese and reserved beans and cook, stirring constantly, for 2-3 minutes or until cheese melts. Serve dip warm with tortilla chips.

TROPICAL CUP

REALLY EASY!

V

A delicious, fruity, non-alcoholic drink.

Makes about 2.5 litres (4 pints)

1 ripe mango, peeled and sliced
1 small melon, peeled and roughly chopped
90g (3 oz) caster sugar
juice of 1 lemon
pulp of 4 passionfruit
500 ml (16 fl oz) orange juice
1.25 litres (3 pints) chilled soda or sparkling mineral water
slices of kiwi fruit
ice cubes

1 Purée mango and melon in a food processor, or push through a sieve.

2 Combine purée with caster sugar and lemon juice. Cover and chill overnight.

3 Stir in the passionfruit pulp, orange juice and chilled soda or mineral water. Decorate with slices of kiwi fruit and ice cubes.

CHAMPAGNE CUP

REALLY EASY!

V

A sparkling Champagne punch ideal for any Christmas party.

Makes 2.5 litres (4 pints)

75 ml (2½ fl oz) brandy
75 ml (2½ fl oz) Cointreau
1 teaspoon angostura bitters
1 tablespoon caster sugar
500 ml (16 fl oz) grape juice
2 bottles chilled Champagne or dry sparkling white wine
ice cubes
small bunches of cherries or grapes

1 Combine the brandy, Cointreau, bitters, caster sugar and grape juice. Cover and chill overnight.

2 Pour into a large jug or punch bowl and stir in Champagne or sparkling wine.

3 Add the ice cubes and decorate edges of jug or punch bowl with cherries or grapes.

35

V

MULLED WINE

REALLY EASY!

Warm red wine with spices and lemon – just the thing to welcome guests on a cold winter's evening.

Makes about 1 litre (1½ pints)

250 ml (8 fl oz) water
1 cinnamon stick
6 whole cloves
6 allspice berries
1 bottle red wine
180 ml (6 fl oz) port
1 tablespoon caster sugar
pared rind of ½ lemon, cut into thin strips
1 lemon, thinly sliced

1 Put the water and spices into a saucepan and simmer, covered, for 20 minutes.

2 Pour the red wine into another saucepan. Strain in spiced water. Reserve spices for garnish if liked.

3 Add the port and sugar to the pan and heat until mixture is almost boiling. Serve hot with lemon peel and lemon slices. Garnish with reserved spices if liked.

STARTERS

The Christmas meal isn't complete without a special first course. Choose from the following delectable starter ideas – there's something for everyone and some of the recipes also make great lunch or supper dishes.

CHESTNUT AND CRANBERRY SOUP

REALLY EASY!

Fresh cranberries are becoming more widely available at Christmas time. Look out for them in the larger supermarkets.

Serves 6

1 tablespoon vegetable oil
1 onion, chopped
2 sticks celery, chopped
900 ml (1½ pints) vegetable stock
bouquet garni
salt and pepper to taste
500g (1 lb) peeled cooked chestnuts, or can unsweetened chestnut purée
60g (2 oz) fresh cranberries
60 ml (2 fl oz) port
parsley sprigs and a few whole cranberries to garnish, (optional)

1 Heat the oil in a saucepan and sauté the onion until softened. Add the celery, stock, bouquet garni and seasoning. Bring to the boil, cover and simmer for 15 minutes.

2 Add the chestnuts and cranberries to the pan and simmer for 15 minutes. Remove and discard the bouquet garni. Allow soup to cool slightly, then blend in a food processor until smooth.

3 Return the soup to the pan, add the port, adjust seasoning heat for 1-2 minutes. Serve garnished with parsley and whole cranberries if liked.

ROQUEFORT AND ALMOND SOUP

REALLY EASY!

A delicious creamy soup of Roquefort, milk and ground almonds.

Serves 4-6

1 tablespoon sunflower oil
1 clove garlic, crushed
1 tablespoon plain flour
600 ml (1 pint) milk
60g (2 oz) ground almonds
60g (2 oz) Roquefort cheese
2 tablespoons chopped chervil or parsley
salt and pepper to taste
croûtons to serve

1 Heat the oil in a saucepan, add the garlic and sauté for 1 minute. Remove from the heat and stir in flour, then 150 ml (5 fl oz) milk.

2 Add the ground almonds to pan then add the remaining milk. Return to the heat and bring to the boil. Cook for 3 minutes or until thickened.

3 Crumble in the Roquefort, add the herbs and cook gently until cheese has melted. Season. Serve with croutons.

STRIPED SALMON TERRINE

EASY!

An impressive-looking starter made from salmon, sole and cream and delicately flavoured with dill and tarragon.

Serves 4-6

350g (12 oz) boned salmon, skinned
1 egg white
150 ml (5 fl oz) double cream
lemon juice to taste
salt and pepper to taste
350g (12 oz) sole fillets, skinned
2 tablespoons chopped fresh dill
1 tablespoon chopped fresh tarragon or parsley
butter for greasing
salad leaves, fresh herb sprigs and crème fraîche, to serve

1 Cut the salmon into 2.5 cm (1 inch) pieces, place in a food processor and blend until smooth. Add egg white and blend again until evenly mixed. Place in refrigerator and chill for at least 30 minutes.

2 Return salmon to food processor and add cream, lemon juice and salt and pepper. Blend until smooth. Chill for 30 minutes.

3 Cut sole fillets into long strips and roll in chopped herbs until well coated.

4 Preheat oven to 180C,350F, Gas 4. Grease a 600 ml (1 pint) loaf tin or terrine with butter. Spoon one third of the salmon mixture into the tin and spread evenly. Lay sole strips on top, leaving a border at each side. Carefully spoon remaining salmon mixture over sole and level the surface.

5 Cover with buttered foil and place in a roasting tin, containing enough hot water to come half-way up the sides of the terrine. Bake in oven for 35 minutes or until a flne skewer inserted into the centre comes out clean.

6 Lift terrine out of roasting tin and leave until cold. Remove foil, cover with oiled greaseproof paper and weight down. Chill for at least 4 hours before turning out. Cut into slices and serve with salad leaves, herb sprigs and crème fraîche.

35

V

CAULIFLOWER AND CRESS SOUP

REALLY EASY!

A flavoursome soup of watercress, onion, cauliflower and cream.

Serves 6

1 bunch watercress
2 tablespoons vegetable oil
1 onion, chopped
1 small cauliflower, chopped
750 ml (1¼ pints) well-flavoured vegetable or chicken stock
salt and pepper to taste
4 tablespoons single cream
crusty bread to serve

1 Roughly chop the watercress. Heat the oil in a saucepan, add onion and watercress, cover and cook gently for about 10 minutes until softened.

2 Add the cauliflower, stock and seasoning. Bring to the boil, cover and simmer gently for 15-20 minutes or until cooked.

3 Cool slightly, then pour into a food processor and blend until smooth. Return to the pan and heat through. Pour into individual serving bowls and swirl in the cream. Serve with crusty bread.

35

OYSTERS WITH GRAVLAX

REALLY EASY!

This recipe can be prepared earlier in the day and kept chilled until required.

Serves 8

250g (8 oz) gravlax or smoked salmon slices
16 oysters in the shell
3 tablespoons lemon juice
freshly ground black pepper

1 Cut gravlax or smoked salmon into long strips. Loosen oysters in their shells.

2 Top oysters with gravlax or smoked salmon slices. Sprinkle with lemon juice and season with black pepper. Cover and refrigerate until required.

35

HAM AND ASPARAGUS GRATINS

EASY!

Serves 4

12 large asparagus spears
6 slices roast ham
30g (1 oz) fresh white breadcrumbs
30g (1 oz) flaked almonds

Sauce

45g (1½ oz) butter
45g (1½ oz) plain flour
450 ml (15 fl oz) milk
90g (3 oz) gruyère or mature Cheddar cheese, grated
2 teaspoons French mustard
salt and pepper to taste

1 For the sauce, melt the butter in a small saucepan. Add flour and cook for 1 minute, stirring. Remove pan from heat and gradually stir in milk. Return to heat and cook, stirring, until smooth. Stir in cheese and mustard and season with salt and pepper. Remove pan from heat.

2 Break off and discard woody ends of asparagus spears. Thinly peel stems using a potato peeler. Cook asparagus in a pan of boiling water for 4 minutes, then drain.

3 Preheat oven to 190C,375F, Gas 5. Cut ham slices in half and wrap each piece around an asparagus stem. Arrange ham and asparagus rolls in a lightly greased baking dish. Spoon over sauce and top with breadcrumbs and almonds. Bake in oven for about 20 minutes until sauce is hot and bubbling and topping is crisp and golden. Serve immediately.

CRISPY BACON AND AVOCADO SALAD

REALLY EASY!

A lovely salad of avocado, salad greens, crisp bacon and chopped hazelnuts, topped with a nutty dressing.

Serves 4

1 avocado
6 rindless rashers of streaky bacon, chopped
250g (8 oz) mixed salad leaves
60g (2 oz) hazelnuts, chopped and toasted

Dressing

3 tablespoons hazelnut oil
1 tablespoon cider vinegar
1 teaspoon French mustard
1 clove garlic, crushed
salt and pepper to taste

1 For the dressing, put all the ingredients in a screw-topped jar and shake to combine.

2 Halve, stone and peel the avocado. Slice into a bowl and pour over the dressing, tossing until coated.

3 Dry-fry the bacon in a non-stick pan until crisp, then add to the avocado. Add the salad leaves and hazelnuts and toss gently until mixed. Serve immediately.

SMOKED SALMON PARCELS

REALLY EASY!

This starter is simplicity itself. Smoked salmon wrapped around a cream cheese filling, tied up with chives and served on a bed of salad leaves.

Serves 4

2 hard-boiled eggs, shelled and finely chopped
125g (4 oz) cream cheese
3 tablespoons double cream
2 teaspoons snipped chives
salt and pepper to taste
4 slices smoked salmon
a few whole chives
125g (4 oz) mixed salad leaves
toast to serve

Dressing

4 tablespoons olive oil
2 tablespoons lemon juice
½ teaspoon French mustard
pinch of sugar

1 Put the eggs, cream cheese, cream and chives into a bowl and mix well. Season with salt and pepper.

2 Lay the smoked salmon slices flat and divide the cream cheese mixture between them. Roll or fold to enclose the fllling. Tie each parcel with whole chives and refrigerate, covered with plastic wrap, until required.

3 For the dressing, put all the ingredients in a screw-topped jar and shake to combine. Season with salt and pepper.

4 Just before serving, put the salad leaves into a bowl, add the dressing and toss gently to mix. Arrange salad leaves on individual plates with the salmon parcels. Serve with toast.

MELON AND PARMA HAM

REALLY EASY!

This recipe gives a twist to the favourite combination of melon and Parma ham by adding a creamy dressing made with dolcelatte cheese.

Serves 4-6

1 small Charentais melon
1 small Galia or Ogen melon
12 very thin slices Parma ham

Dressing

60g (2 oz) dolcelatte cheese
juice of ½ lemon
1-2 teaspoons olive oil
1-2 tablespoons cream or milk
freshly ground black pepper to taste
fresh mint sprigs to garnish

1 Cut the melons into thin wedges and arrange on individual serving plates with the Parma ham. Cover and chill.

2 For the dressing, mash the dolcelatte and lemon juice to a paste, then stir in the olive oil, cream or milk and black pepper to taste.

3 Just before serving, spoon the cheese dressing over the melon and garnish with sprigs of mint.

PEAR AND PROSCIUTTO SALAD

REALLY EASY!

This salad is also delicious made with apples in place of the pears.

Serves 4

3 pears, peeled, cored and quartered
2 tablespoons lemon juice
12 small slices prosciutto or lean ham
100g (3½ oz) mozzarella cheese
freshly ground black pepper
2 tablespoons olive oil
sprigs flat-leaved parsley

1 Brush each pear quarter with lemon juice and wrap in a slice of prosciutto or ham. Using a vegetable peeler, peel off slivers of mozzarella cheese.

2 Arrange three prosciutto- or ham-wrapped pear quarters and some cheese slivers on each serving plate. Season to taste with black pepper, drizzle with oil and garnish with parsley sprigs. Serve immediately.

35

V

MOZZARELLA AND EGG SALAD

REALLY EASY!

If quail's eggs are unavailable, this salad is just as delicious made with hen's eggs. Use 4 hen's eggs, hard-boiled and cut into quarters, in place of the quail's eggs.

Serves 4

300g (10 oz) mozzarella cheese, cut into 2 cm (¾ inch) batons (sticks)
1 bunch (180g/6 oz) watercress, broken into small sprigs
8 hard-boiled quail's eggs, halved

Creamy Dressing

60 ml (2 fl oz) double cream
3 tablespoons mayonnaise
2 tablespoons white wine vinegar
freshly ground black pepper

1 To make the dressing, place the cream, mayonnaise, vinegar and black pepper to taste in a bowl and whisk to combine. Add the cheese batons to the dressing and toss to coat.

2 Arrange the watercress sprigs on individual serving plates or a large serving platter. Top with cheese and quail's eggs and serve immediately.

35 SMOKED TROUT AND CHILLI SALAD STARTER

REALLY EASY!

Flaked smoked trout, chopped mango and fresh coriander tossed in a chilli dressing.

Serves 4

1 smoked trout, skin and head removed
2 ripe mangoes or nectarines, flesh cut into thin strips
30g (1 oz) fresh coriander or flat-leaf parsley sprigs

Chilli Dressing

½-1 tablespoon chilli sauce
1 teaspoon brown sugar
4 tablespoons olive oil
2 tablespoons lemon juice
freshly ground black pepper

1 Remove the bones from the trout and break the flesh into pieces.

2 Arrange the trout, mango or nectarine strips and coriander or parsley on a large serving platter or on individual plates.

3 To make the dressing, place chilli sauce, sugar, oil, lemon juice and black pepper to taste in a screw-topped jar and shake well to combine. Spoon dressing over salad and serve immediately.

MAIN COURSE DISHES

For most people Christmas means roast turkey and all the trimmings and here you will find a foolproof recipe for Perfect Roast Turkey. For those who are vegetarian or who prefer something less traditional, there are lots of delicious festive main course dishes.

PERFECT ROAST TURKEY

EASY!

Serve with a selection of festive vegetables; Bacon-Wrapped Sausages (page 66); Perfect Pan Gravy (page 58); Spicy Cranberry Sauce (page 60) and Bread Sauce (page 59).

Serves 10

4.5 kg (9 lb) turkey (see page 5 for useful information on preparing, cooking and carving the bird)
30g (1 oz) butter, melted
sprigs of fresh rosemary and bay leaves to garnish

Rice And Nut Stuffing

300g (10 oz) cooked brown rice
350g (12 oz) fresh minced pork or pork sausagemeat
15g (½ oz) parsley,finely chopped
60g (2 oz) flaked almonds, toasted
juice of 1 lemon
125g (4 oz) sultanas
1 teaspoon dried mixed herbs
salt and pepper to taste

1 Place all the stuffing ingredients in a large bowl and mix until well combined.

2 Preheat the oven to 190C,375F, Gas 5. Wipe turkey inside and out with damp kitchen paper, then dry.

3 Fill the neck cavity of the turkey with one-third of the stuffing. Do not pack tightly or the skin may split during cooking. Shape remaining stuffing into about 16 balls and place in an ovenproof dish. Chill until ready to cook.

4 Truss the turkey following instructions on page 6.

5 Place the turkey in a large roasting pan. Brush all over with melted butter and season with salt and pepper. Roast in the oven for 2¼-2¾ hours until cooked, covering with foil any parts that brown too quickly. To test if the turkey is cooked, insert a metal skewer into the thickest part of both thighs. When cooked, the juices should run clear with no trace of pink.

6 When cooked, remove turkey from the oven and allow to stand for 20 minutes.

7 Meanwhile, cook the stuffing balls in the oven for 20-25 minutes until cooked and golden, covering with foil if necessary.

8 When ready to serve, remove trussing strings and skewer from turkey and place on a warmed serving plate. Arrange stuffing balls and other accompaniments around the turkey and garnish with fresh herbs.

HONEY-GLAZED HAM

EASY!

A cooked glazed ham makes a wonderful centre-piece for a Christmas buffet.

Serves 20-25

4.5 kg (9 lb) cooked leg of ham, (see page 10)
150g (5 oz) clear honey
250 ml (8 fl oz) fresh orange juice
1 tablespoon French mustard
2 teaspoons soy sauce
1 tablespoon soft brown sugar
whole cloves
watercress to garnish
pickles, mustard and Apricot and Orange Relish (page 61) to serve

1 Preheat the oven to 180C,350F, Gas 4. To remove the skin from the ham, start from the broad end of the ham, and gently ease skin away from the fat. Continue to peel off gently, and the skin should come off in one complete piece.

2 Hold ham firmly in one hand and, with a sharp knife, score the fat in a diamond pattern. Be careful to cut just through the fat, and not into the meat.

3 Place the ham in a large roasting pan. Combine the remaining ingredients, except the cloves, in a bowl, and brush about a quarter of the mixture over ham.

4 Stud each diamond in the fat with a whole clove. Place ham in oven and bake for 1 hour, brushing every 20 minutes with remaining glaze and cooking juices in the roasting pan.

5 If serving the ham hot, allow it to rest for 5 minutes then transfer to a warmed serving plate and garnish with watercress. If serving the ham cold, it may be glazed the day before and refrigerated, but allow to stand at room temperature for 20 minutes before carving. Cold meats are more succulent if not served straight from the fridge. Serve with pickles, mustard and Apricot and Orange Relish.

FRENCH ROAST CHICKEN WITH CREAM GRAVY

Not everyone wants to cook a large turkey at Christmas, so for those who don't here is a chicken recipe which is rather special and ideal for 2-4 servings.

Serves 4

1.5 kg (3 lb) oven-ready chicken
fresh herbs and celery leaves to garnish

Cheese Mixture

90g (3 oz) cream cheese
2 tablespoons fresh chopped parsley
2 teaspoons fresh chopped tarragon or ½ teaspoon dried tarragon leaves
1 small onion, finely chopped
15g (½ oz) butter, softened
salt and pepper to taste

Stuffing

30g (1 oz) butter
1 small onion, finely chopped
2 sticks celery, finely chopped
2 teaspoons fresh chopped tarragon or ½ teaspoon dried tarragon leaves
2 tablespoons fresh chopped parsley
1 teaspoon finely grated lemon rind
125g (4 oz) fresh white breadcrumbs

To Cook Chicken

250 ml (8 fl oz) dry white wine
250 ml (8 fl oz) chicken stock
15g (½ oz) butter

For Gravy

350 ml (12 fl oz) cooking liquid from roasting
extra chicken stock, if necessary
1 tablespoon cornflour, mixed with 125 ml (4 fl oz) single cream
pinch of ground paprika

1 Preheat the oven to 180C,350F, Gas 4. Remove excess fat from the inside of the chicken. Combine the cheese with the parsley, tarragon, onion, butter and salt and pepper. With your fingers, gently ease skin away from chicken breast. Push the cheese mixture over the flesh and re-position the skin on top.

2 For the stuffing, melt the butter in a small saucepan and cook the onion until softened. Combine with remaining stuffing ingredients. Spoon into neck cavity and close cavity with trussing pins.

3 Truss the chicken, see page 6, and place, breast-side up, on a wire rack set in a flameproof roasting pan. Add the wine, stock and butter to pan and roast chicken in the oven for 1¼-1½ hours until crisp and golden and cooked; to test if the chicken is cooked, pierce thickest part of thigh with a skewer. When cooked, the juices will run clear. Baste frequently and turn the chicken 2 or 3 times during cooking. Roast breast-side up for the last 15 minutes.

4 To make the gravy, transfer chicken to a warmed plate to rest for 5 minutes before carving. Place roasting pan on top of cooker and bring liquid in pan to the boil. If necessary, add extra stock to make up to 350 ml (12 fl oz). Stir about 60 ml (2 fl oz) of hot liquid into the cornflour mixture, then stir into pan. Continue stirring until smooth and thickened, and season.

5 Remove trussing pins and strings and carve the chicken into 4 portions. Serve on heated plates with a little gravy spooned over. Serve remaining gravy separately, sprinkled with paprika.

PESTO STUFFED TURKEY FILLETS

EASY!

This recipe uses boneless turkey breast fillet to make carving easier, but you might like to use the traditional whole turkey. You can use one of the stuffings on pages 64 and 65 instead of the pesto stuffing, if desired.

Serves 10

2 x 1 kg (2 lb) boneless turkey breast fillets
125 ml (4 fl oz) water
2 tablespoons sunflower oil

Pesto Stuffing

180g (6 oz) fresh white breadcrumbs
90g (3 oz) butter, melted
1 egg, lightly beaten
3 cloves garlic, crushed
60g (2 oz) fresh grated Parmesan cheese
2 tablespoons finely chopped fresh basil
60g (2 oz) pine nuts, toasted

1 To make the stuffing place the breadcrumbs, butter, egg, garlic, Parmesan cheese, basil and pine nuts in a bowl. Mix well to combine all ingredients.

2 Preheat the oven to 180C,350F, Gas 4. Lay the turkey breasts out flat, skin side down on a large board. Using a sharp knife, cut the breasts horizontally, almost all the way through the centre. Open out breasts and place between two sheets of plastic food wrap. Pound lightly with a rolling pin to flatten slightly.

3 Place the stuffing down the centre of fillet. Roll up to enclose stuffing and secure with toothpicks or tie with string at even intervals.

4 Place on a roasting rack in a baking dish. Pour water into the baking dish and brush the turkey with oil. Cover and bake in the oven for 1¼ hours or until tender and cooked through. Stand covered for 15 minutes before slicing.

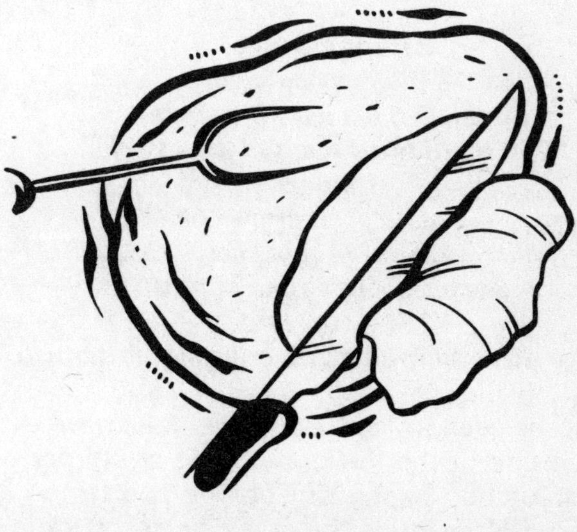

DUCK WITH ORANGE SAUCE

Duck cooked in stock and then drained and roasted and served with an orange, wine and port sauce.

Serves 4

2.5 kg (5 lb) oven-ready duck
1 orange and 1 lemon
salt and pepper to taste
1 small onion, chopped
few stalks of parsley
neck and giblets from duck
500 ml (16 fl oz) water

Orange Sauce

3 tablespoons sugar
60 ml (2 fl oz) red wine vinegar
250 ml (8 fl oz) reserved duck stock
1 orange
1 tablespoon arrowroot
125 ml (4 fl oz) port
2 tablespoons Grand Marnier
15g (½ oz) butter
orange slices and watercress or parsley to garnish

1 Preheat the oven to 180C,350F, Gas 4. Remove excess fat from inside of the duck, and wipe cavity dry with absorbent kitchen paper. Cut orange and lemon into quarters and place inside the cavity. Season duck inside and out with salt and pepper, and truss, see page 6.

2 Place duck in a deep casserole dish with onion, parsley, roughly chopped neck and giblets and water. Cover the casserole and cook duck in the oven for 1 hour, turning once or twice.

3 Remove duck, reserving the liquid, and place breast-side up on a rack in a roasting pan. Increase oven temperature to 190C,375F, Gas 5. Return duck to oven and roast, uncovered, for 10 minutes, turn breast-side down and roast another 10 minutes, or until duck is golden brown.

4 Meanwhile, to make the sauce, strain the liquid from the casserole dish and skim as much fat as possible from the surface. Reserve 250 ml (8 fl oz). Place sugar and vinegar in a saucepan. Boil for a minute or two until thick and syrupy. Stir in reserved stock.

5 To make the sauce carefully remove rind from orange with a vegetable peeler and cut into fine strips. Add to saucepan and bring to a simmer. Squeeze juice from orange and mix with the arrowroot. Add to the sauce and stir until smooth and thick.

6 Stir in the port and Grand Marnier. Heat through but do not boil. Season to taste with salt and pepper and stir in the butter.

7 Remove trussing strings from duck and place on a warmed serving dish. Spoon a little sauce over to glaze and serve the rest separately in a sauce boat. Garnish platter with orange slices and watercress or parsley.

ROAST FILLET OF BEEF WITH PORT AND NUT STUFFING

EASY!

Fillet of beef with an orange and nut stuffing served with a rich port gravy.
If preferred, you can vary the stuffing ingredients with whatever you have available. Replace the walnuts with Brazil nuts, cashew nuts or pine nuts; the parsley with tarragon or mixed herbs; the orange rind with lemon rind and the white breadcrumbs with wholemeal breadcrumbs. You may need to add a little extra liquid if using wholemeal crumbs.

Serves 8

1.5 kg (3 lb) fillet of beef, in one piece
watercress to garnish

Stuffing

30g (1 oz) walnuts, coarsely chopped
30g (1 oz) butter, melted
2 tablespoons chopped parsley
2 tablespoons clear honey
1 tablespoon grated orange rind
60 ml (2 fl oz) port
1 egg, beaten
salt and pepper to taste
about 125g (4 oz) fresh white breadcrumbs

To Cook Beef

1 large carrot, coarsely chopped
3 sticks celery, coarsely chopped
1 large onion, coarsely chopped
30g (1 oz) butter

Gravy

250 ml (8 fl oz) beef stock
125 ml (4 fl oz) port

1 Preheat the oven to 200C,400F, Gas 6. Trim the beef, removing all fat and sinews. Make a lengthwise incision to form a pocket for stuffing, cutting only three-quarters of the way through.

2 Combine all the stuffing ingredients, adding enough breadcrumbs to make a stuffing that is moist, but not wet.

3 Fill the pocket with stuffing and tie beef at 5 cm (2 inch) intervals with fine string to keep stuffing in place.

4 Scatter carrots, celery and onion in the base of a roasting pan and dot with butter. Place beef on top of vegetables. Roast in the oven for 50-60 minutes for medium-rare beef, turning beef half-way through cooking time. Remove beef to a warmed serving plate, cover loosely with foil and allow to rest for about 15 minutes before carving.

5 Strain the pan juices through a sieve into a saucepan, pressing down on vegetables to extract as much liquid as possible. Add beef stock and port to the saucepan and bring to the boil. Boil rapidly until liquid is reduced to thin gravy consistency. Season to taste with salt and pepper.

6 Remove strings from beef. Spoon a little gravy over the beef and garnish with watercress. Carve beef into neat, thick slices and serve remaining gravy separately in a warmed sauce boat.

REDCURRANT LAMB ROAST

REALLY EASY!

Roast leg of lamb made festive by the addition of a redcurrant jelly sauce.

Serves 6

1.5 kg (3 lb) lean leg lamb

To Baste

30g butter
1 teaspoon grated fresh root ginger
1 clove garlic, crushed
1 teaspoon soy sauce
1 tablespoon redcurrant jelly

Sauce

2 tablespoons redcurrant jelly
250 ml (8 fl oz) chicken stock
2 tablespoons chopped fresh mint
1 tablespoon cornflour blended with 3 tablespoons port

1 Preheat the oven to 180C,350F, Gas 4. Trim meat of excess fat and place in a baking dish. To make basting sauce, combine butter, ginger, garlic, soy sauce and redcurrant jelly in a saucepan. Stir over medium heat until butter melts.

2 Pour over lamb and bake in the oven for 1¼-1½ hours until cooked as desired, basting frequently with pan liquid. Remove meat and keep warm.

3 To make sauce, place baking dish on top of stove. Combine redcurrant jelly, stock and mint. Bring to the boil, whisk in blended cornflour, stirring until sauce thickens. Slice meat and serve with the sauce.

CHEESY BROWN RICE PIE

REALLY EASY!

V **A savoury pie of brown rice, cheese, courgettes, red pepper, asparagus, eggs and yogurt.**

Serves 6

180g (6 oz) brown rice, cooked
250g (8 oz) grated cheese
4 tablespoons grated Parmesan cheese
2 spring onions, chopped
2 courgettes, grated
1 red pepper, seeded and diced
300g (10 oz) canned asparagus tips, drained
3 tablespoons pine nuts, toasted
3 eggs, lightly beaten
200g (7 oz) natural yogurt
freshly ground black pepper

1 Preheat oven to 190C,375F, Gas 5. Place rice, cheese, Parmesan cheese, spring onions, courgettes, red pepper, asparagus, pine nuts, eggs, yogurt and black pepper to taste in a bowl and mix gently to combine.

2 Spoon the rice mixture into a greased, deep-sided 23 cm (9 inch) springform tin and bake in the oven for 40 minutes or until firm. Allow to stand for 5 minutes in tin before turning out and serving. Serve cut into wedges.

VEGETARIAN FILO SLICE

V

Whether you are a vegetarian or simply want something a little bit different to serve over the festive period, try this delicious layered vegetable filo slice.

Serves 6-8

350g (12 oz) broccoli, cut into large pieces
500g (1 lb) carrots, roughly sliced
125g (4 oz) split red lentils
30g (1 oz) butter
1 onion, roughly chopped
2 cloves garlic, crushed
125g (4 oz) ground almonds
60g (2 oz) mature Cheddar cheese, grated
4 eggs
1 red pepper, seeded and finely chopped
salt and pepper to taste
½ teaspoon curry powder
30g (1 oz) fresh breadcrumbs
5 sheets filo pastry
oil for brushing
whole red chillies, parsley sprigs and Parmesan cheese to garnish

Sauce

1 red pepper, seeded and chopped
2 cloves garlic, crushed
½ green or red chilli, seeded and sliced
15g (½ oz) fresh breadcrumbs
5 tablespoons olive oil

1 Preheat the oven to 180C,350F, Gas 4. Grease and line a 1 kg (2 lb) loaf tin with greased greaseproof or non-stick baking paper.

2 Cook the broccoli in a saucepan of boiling water until just cooked, drain well. Cook carrots in a separate pan of boiling water for 10 minutes. Add lentils to carrots and cook for a further 10 minutes, drain well.

3 Melt butter in a pan and cook onion and garlic for 3 minutes. Place onions in a food processor and blend with broccoli and ground almonds to a smooth purée. Put into a bowl and add the cheese and 2 of the eggs. Beat until combined then stir in red pepper and seasoning. Turn into the prepared tin.

4 Blend carrots and lentils with remaining 2 eggs, curry powder, breadcrumbs and seasoning. Spoon into the tin. Using a teaspoon lightly swirl the two mixtures together. Cover with foil and bake in the oven for 1 hour. Cool, then remove from tin.

5 Wrap the loaf, like a parcel, in a sheet of pastry. Brush with oil and wrap with 3 more sheets of pastry, brushing each with oil.

6 Transfer the loaf to a baking sheet. Lay remaining sheet of pastry over loaf, easing pastry into soft folds. Brush lightly with oil and bake at 180C,350F, Gas 4 for 40 minutes, covering with foil once the pastry has turned golden.

7 Meanwhile make the sauce. Place red pepper, garlic, chilli and breadcrumbs in a blender and blend to a paste. Add the oil and blend until smooth.

8 Transfer loaf to a warmed serving plate. Serve sliced with the sauce and garnish with chillies, parsley and Parmesan.

SPICY VEGETABLE LOAF

REALLY EASY!

V

A spicy loaf made with lentils, oats, tomatoes carrot and potato.

Serves 6

1 tablespoon olive oil
1 clove garlic, crushed
1 onion, chopped
½ teaspoon chilli powder
½ teaspoon ground cumin
½ teaspoon ground coriander
½ teaspoon ground turmeric
500g (1 lb) red lentils
1 carrot, grated
1 large potato, grated
400g (14 oz) can chopped tomatoes, undrained and mashed
500 ml (16 fl oz) vegetable stock
3 egg whites
150g (5 oz) rolled oats
freshly ground black pepper

1 Heat the oil in a large frying pan, add the garlic, onion, chilli powder, cumin, coriander and turmeric and cook for 4-5 minutes or until onion is soft.

2 Add the lentils, carrot, potato, tomatoes and stock and bring to the boil. Reduce heat, cover and simmer for 30 minutes or until lentils are tender. Remove pan from heat and set aside to cool slightly.

3 Preheat oven to 180C,350F, Gas 4. Place the egg whites in a bowl and beat until stiff peaks form. Fold egg whites into lentil mixture.

4 Stir rolled oats into lentil mixture and season to taste with black pepper. Spoon into a lightly greased 11x21 cm (4½ x 8½ inch) loaf tin and bake in the oven for 1 hour.

SAUCES, STUFFINGS AND ACCOMPANIMENTS

It's the extra trimmings and sauces that make the Christmas meal so special. On the following pages you will find ideas for sauces and stuffings that can be used either with the traditional turkey meal or to accompany something less conventional.

PERFECT PAN GRAVY

REALLY EASY!

A delicious pan gravy to accompany the Perfect Roast Turkey (page 40).

Makes about 1.1 litres (1¾ pints)

giblets and neck from turkey
1 bay leaf
5-6 black peppercorns
few onion slices
few fresh parsley stalks
salt and pepper to taste
1.2 litres (2 pints) water
4-5 tablespoons roasting juices from cooking turkey
4 tablespoons plain flour

1 Place giblets and neck, bay leaf, peppercorns, onion, parsley, salt and water in a saucepan. Bring to the boil, then simmer for 1 hour. Strain, then reserve liquid.

2 Heat cooking juices from turkey in roasting pan over a gentle heat. Sprinkle over the flour and stir with a wooden spoon until smooth.

3 Continue cooking and stirring until mixture turns a light golden colour. Gradually stir in reserved liquid. Increase heat to moderate and stir until gravy comes to the boil and is smooth and thickened.

4 Adjust seasoning. Pour into a warmed gravy boat.

35

V

BREAD SAUCE

REALLY EASY!

A traditional sauce to serve with turkey or chicken, made with onion-flavoured milk, breadcrumbs and cream.

Makes about 500 ml (16 fl oz)

6 whole cloves
1 onion, peeled
1 bay leaf
600 ml (1 pint) milk
90-125g (3-4 oz) fresh white breadcrumbs
60g (2 oz) butter
salt and pepper to taste
large pinch ground nutmeg
2 tablespoons single cream

1 Stick cloves into the onion. Put onion, bay leaf and milk in a saucepan and bring to the boil. Remove from heat, then cover and set aside for 30 minutes.

2 Add breadcrumbs and butter to the milk in the pan. Cook sauce over a very gentle heat for 15-20 minutes. Remove the onion and bay leaf and add seasoning and nutmeg. Stir in cream just before serving.

SPICY CRANBERRY SAUCE

REALLY EASY!

A lovely tangy sauce that can be served with hot or cold turkey or chicken.

Makes about 250 ml (8 fl oz)

300g (10 oz) bottled cranberry sauce
1 teaspoon finely chopped fresh root ginger
1 teaspoon ground cardamom
½ teaspoon ground cinnamon
2 teaspoons Worcestershire sauce

1 Place all ingredients in a small saucepan. Stir until mixture boils, then simmer for 1 minute. Allow to cool.

2 Store in an airtight container in the refrigerator. Serve with turkey or other poultry.

CUMBERLAND SAUCE

REALLY EASY!

Made with redcurrant jelly, marmalade, orange and lemon juice and port, this is an ideal addition to cooked gammon or ham.

Makes about 125 ml (4 fl oz)

4 tablespoons redcurrant jelly
1 tablespoon marmalade
juice of 1 orange and ½ lemon
75 ml (2½ fl oz) port

1 Melt the redcurrant jelly in a small saucepan over low heat. Stir in the marmalade, orange and lemon juice, and port. Simmer for 1 minute.

2 Remove from heat and cool. Store in an airtight container in the refrigerator. Serve with pork or ham.

35

V

APRICOT AND ORANGE RELISH

REALLY EASY!

A fruity relish ideal to serve with cooked gammon or ham and even pork.

180g (6 oz) dried ready-to-eat apricots
300 ml (10 fl oz) unsweetened orange juice
2 tablespoons white wine vinegar
1 tablespoon clear honey
1 teaspoon cornflour
salt and pepper to taste
pinch of ground nutmeg or ginger

1 Place the apricots in a saucepan with the orange juice, vinegar and honey. Bring the mixture to the boil, then simmer gently for 5 minutes until soft and pulpy.

2 Blend apricot mixture in a food processor until smooth, then transfer to a small pan and stir in the cornflour.

3 Reheat mixture gently, stirring continuously until thickened. Season with salt and pepper and nutmeg or ginger. Serve relish hot or cold.

GINGER AND LIME SAUCE

REALLY EASY!

An unusual sauce made with garlic, ginger, lime marmalade and Madeira – wonderful with roast chicken.

15g (½ oz) butter
3 cloves garlic, finely sliced
2 teaspoons grated fresh root ginger
350ml (12 fl oz) stock, made from strained pan juices and chicken stock
4 tablespoons lime marmalade
125 ml (4 fl oz) Madeira
1½ tablespoons cornflour blended with 3 tablespoons water

1 Melt the butter in a saucepan and cook the garlic and ginger for 1-2 minutes. Stir in stock and cook over medium heat until mixture boils. Reduce heat and simmer for 10 minutes.

2 Strain mixture to remove garlic and ginger, then return to pan. Add lime marmalade and cornflour mixture and cook over a medium heat, stirring frequently until sauce boils and thickens.

35

OATY STUFFING BALLS

REALLY EASY!

Pork sausagemeat balls coated in herbs and oatmeal and baked in the oven.

Serves 8

500g (1 lb) pork sausagemeat
1 onion,finely chopped
salt and pepper to taste
90g (3 oz) medium ground oatmeal
2 teaspoons dried mixed herbs
salt and pepper to taste

1 Preheat oven to 190C,375F, Gas 5. Put sausagemeat, onion and salt and pepper into a bowl and mix until well combined.

2 Shape stuffing into 16 small balls. Mix oatmeal with herbs and seasoning. Spread out on a plate and roll stuffing balls in oatmeal mixture.

3 Place stuffing balls in a greased ovenproof dish and bake for 20-25 minutes.

35

RAISIN, APPLE AND GINGER STUFFING

REALLY EASY!

A stuffing of breadcrumbs and minced pork with apple, raisins, ginger, honey and cinnamon.

Serves 4-6

180g (6 oz) fresh white breadcrumbs
90g (3 oz) butter, melted
1 egg, lightly beaten
30g (1 oz) dried apple, roughly chopped
3 tablespoons raisins, chopped
2 tablespoons grated fresh root ginger
2 tablespoons honey
¼ teaspoon ground cinnamon
125g (4 oz) fresh minced pork

1 Place breadcrumbs, butter, egg, apple, raisins, ginger, honey, cinnamon and pork in a bowl and mix well to combine. Use as required.

35

FIG AND PECAN STUFFING

V

REALLY EASY!

A stuffing of breadcrumbs, celery, figs, pecans, parsley and spices.

Serves 4-6

1 tablespoon vegetable oil
1 medium onion, chopped
180g (6 oz) soft white breadcrumbs
90g (3 oz) butter, melted
1 egg, lightly beaten
2 sticks celery, finely sliced
150g (5 oz) chopped dried figs
90g (3 oz) pecan nuts, chopped
2 tablespoons finely chopped fresh parsley
2 teaspoons ground cardamom
3 teaspoons ground coriander
2 teaspoons ground ginger
freshly ground black pepper

1 Heat the oil in a frying pan and cook the onion for 4-5 minutes or until golden.

2 Place breadcrumbs, butter, egg, onion, celery, figs, pecans, parsley, cardamom, coriander, ginger and pepper in a bowl and mix well to combine. Use as required.

35

BACON-WRAPPED SAUSAGES

REALLY EASY!

If preferred these bacon-wrapped sausages can be cooked under a preheated grill for about 5 minutes. As an alternative to sausages, wrap bacon around ready-to-eat dried prunes or cooked chestnuts.

Serves 8

8 rashers of streaky bacon, rinds removed
16 small chipolata sausages

1 Preheat the oven to 190C,375F, Gas 5. Hold each bacon rasher with one hand, and stretch it with the back of a knife. Cut the rasher in half.

2 Roll a half-rasher of bacon around each sausage. Place join-side down in a roasting pan and cook in the oven for 20-25 minutes until cooked.

VEGETABLES

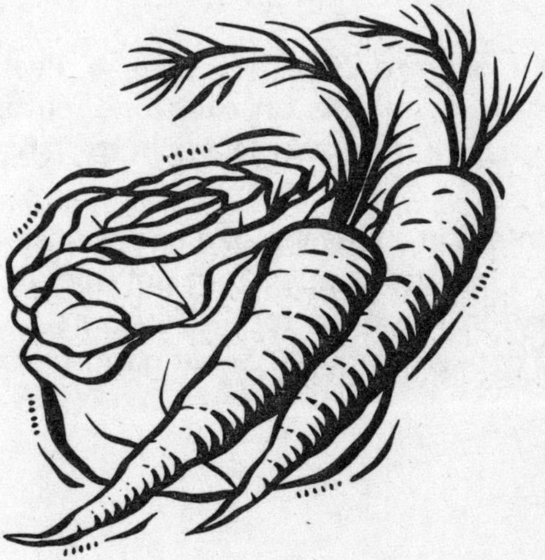

Ring the changes this Christmas and try some of these unusual and tasty vegetable ideas. Most of the recipes are quite simple so they will complement a rich main course and some that include a sauce will go well with cold meats.

ROSEMARY POTATOES

REALLY EASY!

Roast potatoes with a touch of rosemary.

Serves 6

1 kg (2 lb) small old potatoes
4-5 sprigs fresh rosemary
3 tablespoons olive oil
coarse sea salt and freshly ground black pepper to taste
fresh rosemary sprigs to garnish

1 Preheat the oven to 200C,400F, Gas 6. Peel the potatoes and make deep cuts on each one, cutting almost right through. Strip rosemary leaves from stalks and chop them.

2 Place potatoes in a roasting pan and sprinkle with rosemary, oil and salt and pepper. Turn potatoes to coat thoroughly. Bake in the oven for 1-$1\frac{1}{4}$ hours until golden brown and cooked through. Serve garnished with rosemary.

35

V

BEANS WITH TOMATO

REALLY EASY!

French beans tossed with olive oil and chopped tomatoes.

Serves 4

500g (1 lb) French beans
3 tablespoons olive oil
2 ripe tomatoes, skinned and chopped
salt and pepper

1 Top and tail the French beans, then rinse and drain. Cook beans in a saucepan of boiling salted water for 7-10 minutes until just tender. Drain well.

2 Heat the oil in a pan, add the tomatoes and cook gently for about 5 minutes. Add beans and stir well. Season. Cover and cook for 2-3 minutes.

ALMOND BRUSSELS SPROUTS

REALLY EASY!

If preferred, replace flaked almonds with 90g (3 oz) cooked whole chestnuts which have been sautéed in a little butter.

Serves 4

500g (1 lb) small Brussels sprouts
30g (1 oz) butter
30g (1 oz) flaked almonds
1 clove garlic, crushed
1 teaspoon finely grated lemon rind
1 teaspoon lemon juice
salt and pepper to taste

1 Trim stalks off sprouts and make a cross in the base of each one. Cook in a saucepan of boiling salted water for 4-5 minutes until just cooked. Drain and keep warm.

2 Meanwhile, melt butter in a small frying pan, add the flaked almonds and garlic and sauté until almonds are golden. Stir in lemon rind and juice and salt and pepper. Mix well.

3 Sprinkle almond mixture over sprouts and stir gently to mix. Serve immediately.

35

V

CRISPY LEEKS

REALLY EASY!

Cooked leeks topped with a wine and mustard sauce and crisp breadcrumbs.

Serves 4

750g (1½ lb) leeks
1 bouquet garni
2 whole cloves
15g (½ oz) butter
125 ml (4 fl oz) vegetable stock
5 tablespoons dry white wine
salt and pepper to taste
1 tablespoon French mustard
1 tablespoon dried brown breadcrumbs

1 Wash leeks and cut into 4 cm (1½ inch) lengths. Place leeks in a saucepan with bouquet garni, cloves, butter, stock, wine and salt and pepper. Bring to the boil, cover and cook for 12-15 minutes until leeks are just cooked. Drain leeks, reserving cooking liquid.

2 Strain cooking liquid back into pan, then boil to reduce by half. Arrange leeks in a buttered shallow ovenproof dish. Add mustard to reduced cooking juices, stir well and pour over the leeks.

3 Preheat grill to moderately hot. Sprinkle breadcrumbs over leeks and grill until topping is crisp and golden.

RATATOUILLE

REALLY EASY!

V

A colourful dish of aubergines, red onions, green peppers, tomatoes, mushrooms and parsley.

Serves 6

2 aubergines, cut into strips
salt
2 tablespoons olive oil
2 large red onions, sliced
2 cloves garlic, crushed
2 green peppers, seeded and sliced
400g (14 oz) can chopped tomatoes, undrained and mashed
4 tablespoons dry white wine
1 tablespoon chopped fresh oregano or 1 teaspoon dried oregano
1 tablespoon tomato purée
250g (8 oz) mushrooms, sliced
3 tablespoons chopped fresh parsley
freshly ground black pepper

1 Place aubergines in a colander set over a bowl and sprinkle with salt. Set aside to stand for 30 minutes, then rinse under cold running water and pat dry with absorbent kitchen paper.

2 Heat the oil in a large frying pan and cook the onions, garlic and green peppers over a medium heat for 3-4 minutes or until onions are soft. Add aubergines, tomatoes, wine, oregano and tomato purée and cook, stirring, over a medium heat for 25-30 minutes or until mixture reduces and thickens.

3 Stir in the mushrooms and cook for 5 minutes longer. Add parsley and season to taste with black pepper. Serve hot, warm or at room temperature.

35

V

SPICY CARROTS WITH CASHEW NUTS

REALLY EASY!

Try this adaptation of an Indian recipe – it is a wonderful way of cooking and serving carrots.

Serves 4

2 tablespoons sunflower oil
500g (1 lb) carrots, peeled and cut lengthways into thick strips
1 large onion, sliced
1 teaspoon grated fresh root ginger
1 teaspoon garam masala
½ teaspoon chilli powder
1 tablespoon plain flour
90g (3 oz) cashew nuts, halved
250 ml (8 fl oz) vegetable or chicken stock

1 Heat oil in a heavy-based saucepan. Add carrots and onion and cook for 5 minutes. Stir in ginger, garam masala, chilli powder, flour, cashews and stock. Cook over medium heat until mixture thickens. Reduce heat.

2 Simmer over low heat for 15-20 minutes, stirring from time to time, or until carrots are tender. Stir frequently during cooking.

35

V

CAULIFLOWER AND BLUE CHEESE GRATIN

REALLY EASY!

Cauliflower and celery coated in a white sauce and topped with a mixture of blue cheese, Parmesan and breadcrumbs.

Serves 4

½ cauliflower, cut into small florets
4 sticks celery, roughly chopped

Sauce

30g (1 oz)butter
1 tablespoon plain flour
250 ml (8 fl oz) milk
2 shallots, finely chopped

Topping

125g (4 oz) blue cheese, crumbled
2 slices multigrain bread, crumbed
freshly ground black pepper
2 tablespoons fresh grated Parmesan cheese

1 Boil, steam or microwave the cauliflower and celery until just tender. Drain and transfer to a shallow ovenproof dish.

2 To make the sauce, melt the butter in a small saucepan, add the flour and cook for 1 minute. Gradually stir in milk and cook over medium heat until sauce boils. Mix in shallots and pour over the vegetables.

3 To make the topping, combine blue cheese, breadcrumbs and pepper and spread over the vegetables. Top with Parmesan cheese and cook under a preheated grill for 5 minutes or until top is golden and crisp.

PARSNIPS BAKED IN SOUR CREAM

V

REALLY EASY!

Sliced parsnips cooked in a sauce of onion, mustard and sour cream.

Serves 4

1 tablespoon sunflower oil
1 large onion, chopped
3 large parsnips, peeled and thickly sliced
250 ml (8 fl oz) vegetable stock
½ teaspoon prepared hot mustard
½ teaspoon paprika
125ml (4 fl oz) sour cream
1 tablespoon plain flour
2 slices wholegrain bread, made into crumbs

1 Preheat the oven to 180C,350F, Gas 4.

2 Heat the oil in a frying pan and cook the onion for 4-5 minutes until soft. Add the parsnips and cook for 4-5 minutes. Combine stock, mustard and paprika. Stir into parsnips and bring to the boil. Reduce heat and simmer for 15 minutes. Mix together sour cream and flour. Remove parsnips from heat and whisk in sour cream mixture.

3 Transfer to a shallow ovenproof dish and sprinkle with the breadcrumbs. Bake in the oven for 30 minutes or until parsnips are tender and the top is golden.

35

V

BROCCOLI IN GINGER SOY SAUCE

REALLY EASY!

Fresh root ginger freezes well. When you want to use it, simply grate the required amount off the piece of frozen ginger.

Serves 4

1 tablespoon vegetable oil
large head broccoli, broken into florets
freshly ground black pepper

Ginger Soy Sauce

1 tablespoon soy sauce
1 tablespoon grated fresh root ginger
2 teaspoons cornflour blended with 125 ml (4 fl oz) vegetable stock or water

1 Heat the oil in a wok or frying pan, add the broccoli and stir-fry for 2-3 minutes or until broccoli changes colour.

2 To make the sauce, combine soy sauce, ginger and cornflour mixture. Pour over broccoli in pan and cook, stirring, for 2-3 minutes or until sauce thickens. Season to taste with black pepper and serve immediately.

CAULIFLOWER WITH PUFFY CHEESE TOPPING

REALLY EASY!

If your sauce has turned lumpy remove it from the heat and beat briskly with a wire balloon whisk or process in a food processor until smooth. Add more liquid if too thick and reheat.

Serves 4

1 medium cauliflower, cut into florets

Sauce

30g (1 oz) butter
1 tablespoon plain flour
250 ml (8 fl oz) milk

Hot Cheese Topping

2 egg whites
2 tablespoons mayonnaise
2 teaspoons sweet chilli sauce
60g (2 oz) grated Cheddar cheese

1 Drop cauliflower florets into a saucepan of boiling water and cook for 8-10 minutes or until just tender. Drain and transfer to a greased ovenproof dish. Preheat the oven to 200C,400F, Gas 6.

2 To make the sauce, melt butter in a saucepan, add flour and cook for 1 minute. Blend in milk, stirring over the heat until sauce boils and thickens. Pour sauce over cauliflower.

3 To make the topping, beat the egg whites until stiff peaks form. Fold through combined mayonnaise and chilli sauce. Spoon over cauliflower mixture. Top with cheese. Bake in the oven for 10-15 minutes or until puffed and golden.

HOT COLESLAW WITH BRANDY DRESSING

REALLY EASY!

Shredded white cabbage with chopped apple and crisp bacon served warm with an oil, vinegar and brandy dressing.

Serves 6

2 rindless bacon rashers, chopped
½ medium white cabbage, shredded
2 green apples, cored and coarsely chopped
½ teaspoon ground nutmeg

Brandy Dressing

1 clove garlic, crushed
1 tablespoon cider vinegar
2 tablespoons brandy
4 tablespoons walnut oil
freshly ground black pepper

1 Cook bacon in a heavy-based frying pan until just crisp. Add the cabbage and apples and toss well. Cook for 3-4 minutes then mix in nutmeg. Using a slotted spoon transfer to a warmed bowl and toss to combine.

2 To make the brandy dressing, combine garlic, vinegar, brandy, oil and pepper in a screw-topped jar and shake well. Pour dressing over coleslaw and serve.

35

V

THREE-CABBAGE STIR-FRY

REALLY EASY!

A speedy stir-fry of red, Chinese and savoy cabbage flavoured with garlic, ginger, chilli and sesame seeds.

Serves 6

1 tablespoon vegetable oil
1 tablespoon sesame oil
1 clove garlic, crushed
1 teaspoon grated fresh root ginger
1 red chilli, seeded and chopped
1 tablespoon sesame seeds
¼ red cabbage, shredded
¼ Chinese cabbage, shredded
¼ savoy cabbage, shredded

1 Heat the vegetable and sesame oils in a wok or frying pan until very hot. Add the garlic, ginger, chilli and sesame seeds and stir-fry for 1 minute.

2 Toss in the cabbages and stir-fry for 3-4 minutes or until just cooked. The cabbages should still retain their colours and be crisp. Serve immediately.

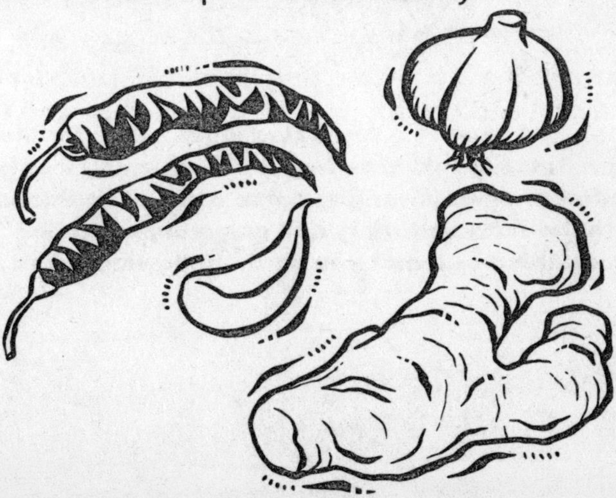

SALADS

It's good to have a few salad ideas ready for the Christmas break. Whether you're planning a cold buffet or simply wanting some unusual additions to the leftover turkey and gammon, you'll find something to tempt you on the following pages.

35

V

BEETROOT SALAD

REALLY EASY!

The cooked and raw beetroot in this salad have quite different textures and make a very interesting combination. Tossed in light dressing, it makes an unusual side dish.

Serves 6

1 large cooked beetroot, grated
1 large raw beetroot, grated
2 green apples, cored and cut into thin strips
fresh sprigs of dill

Dressing

2 tablespoons lemon juice
4 tablespoons sunflower oil
1 tablespoon finely chopped fresh dill
freshly ground black pepper

1 Place beetroot and apples in a salad bowl.

2 To make dressing, combine lemon juice, oil, dill and pepper in a screw-topped jar. Shake well and pour over beetroot and apples. Toss to coat ingredients and serve garnished with dill.

CARROTS AND APPLES

REALLY EASY!

This delicious raw salad, which is especially popular with children, can be served as it is or sprinkled with a little vinaigrette to give extra zing.

Serves 4

2 green apples, cored and grated
juice 1 lemon
2 carrots, scrubbed and grated

1 Toss apples in lemon juice. Place in salad bowl and mix in carrots.

CRUNCHY MANGETOUT SALAD

REALLY EASY!

You might like to use both alfalfa and mung bean sprouts to give added flavour and texture to the salad.

Serves 4

200g (7 oz) trimmed mangetout
1 small lettuce
200g (7 oz) bean sprouts
1 tomato skinned, seeded and cut into strips

Dressing

3 tablespoons vegetable oil
½ teaspoon sesame oil
1 tablespoon soy sauce
1 tablespoon cider vinegar
1 teaspoon grated fresh root ginger
freshly ground black pepper

1 Blanch the mangetout and refresh under cold running water and drain.

2 Line a salad bowl with lettuce leaves. Arrange the mangetout, bean sprouts and tomato strips over the lettuce.

3 To make the dressing, place vegetable oil, sesame oil, soy sauce, vinegar, ginger and pepper in a screw-topped jar. Shake well to combine and pour over salad.

FENNEL AND RED ONION SALAD

REALLY EASY!

Sliced fennel and red onion in a red wine vinegar dressing.

Serves 6

4 heads fennel, trimmed, halved and sliced
1 large red onion, sliced
6 sprigs fresh parsley, finely chopped

Red Wine Vinegar Dressing

125 ml (4 fl oz) olive oil
3 tablespoons red wine vinegar
freshly ground black pepper

1 To make the dressing, place oil and vinegar in a screw-topped jar. Season to taste with pepper. Shake well to combine.

2 Place fennel, onion and parsley in salad bowl. Pour over dressing and toss to combine.

ITALIAN BEAN SALAD

REALLY EASY!

A substantial salad of various beans, avocado, cucumber, salami and anchovies tossed in vinaigrette.

Serves 6-8

500g (1 lb) trimmed green beans, cut into 5 cm (2 inch) pieces
1 avocado, peeled and stone removed
½ cucumber, peeled
300g (10 oz) can three bean mixture, drained
200g (7 oz) salami, cut into strips
60g (2 oz) can anchovy fillets, drained and roughly chopped
250 ml (8 fl oz) vinaigrette dressing
60g (2 oz) piece Parmesan cheese
freshly ground black pepper

1 Boil, steam or microwave the green beans until tender-crisp. Refresh under cold running water and drain. Cut avocado and cucumber into bite-size chunks.

2 In a large salad bowl, combine avocado, cucumber, canned and green beans, salami and anchovies. Toss in vinaigrette dressing and chill.

3 Before serving, coarsely grate Parmesan across the salad and season liberally with freshly ground black pepper.

35

V

ROAST PEPPER SALAD

REALLY EASY!

A very colourful salad of mixed peppers with a garlic and basil dressing.

Serves 6-8

2 red peppers
2 green peppers
2 yellow peppers
freshly ground black pepper

Dressing

12 fresh basil leaves, chopped
1 clove garlic, crushed
125 ml (4 fl oz) olive oil
3 tablespoons red wine vinegar

1 Preheat the oven to 200C,400F, Gas 6. Place the peppers in a baking dish and bake in the oven for 10 minutes. Remove skins and seeds, cut into strips and place in a bowl.

2 To make the dressing, combine basil, garlic, oil and vinegar in a screw-topped jar and shake well to combine. Pour over peppers and toss. Season with pepper and refrigerate until required.

TOMATO BASIL SALAD

REALLY EASY!

Ever popular, this salad adds colour and flavour to any meal. Use fresh young basil leaves, or you might like to use mint leaves to create a Tomato Mint Salad.

Serves 4

2 large tomatoes, sliced
60g (2 oz) fresh basil leaves
1 red onion, sliced into rings

Garlic Dressing

2 cloves garlic, crushed
2 teaspoons olive oil
1 tablespoon fresh lime or lemon juice
freshly ground black pepper

1 Cut each tomato slice in half and arrange alternately with basil leaves on a large serving platter. Place onion rings in centre of platter.

2 To make the dressing, place garlic, oil, lime or lemon juice and black pepper to taste in a screw-topped jar and shake well to combine. Drizzle over salad.

MUSTARD POTATO SALAD

REALLY EASY!

Tiny new potatoes in a sour cream and mustard dressing.

Serves 6

1 kg (2 lb) baby new potatoes, scrubbed

Mustard Dressing

3 tablespoons sour cream
3 tablespoons mayonnaise
2 tablespoons wholegrain mustard
2 tablespoons Dijon mustard

1 Boil the potatoes until tender. Drain, refresh under cold running water, drain again and refrigerate until ready to serve.

2 To make the dressing, place sour cream, mayonnaise, wholegrain and Dijon mustards in a bowl and mix to combine. Place potatoes in a salad bowl, spoon over dressing and serve.

35

V

VEGETABLE SLAW WITH PESTO DRESSING

REALLY EASY!

A crunchy coleslaw of cabbage, carrot, celery, radishes, green pepper and broccoli topped with a mayonnaise and yogurt dressing.

Serves 6

½ savoy cabbage, shredded
1 large carrot, cut into thin strips
4 spring onions, chopped
1 stick celery, cut into thin strips
8 radishes, sliced
1 green pepper, seeded and cut into strips
150g (5 oz) broccoli florets, cooked

Dressing

100g (3½ oz) fresh basil leaves, roughly chopped
2 cloves garlic, crushed
2 tablespoons pine nuts, toasted
2 tablespoons grated Parmesan cheese
5 tablespoons mayonnaise
3 tablespoons natural yogurt

1 Put cabbage, carrot, spring onions, celery, radishes, pepper and broccoli in a salad bowl. Toss lightly, cover and refrigerate until required.

2 To make the dressing, place basil, garlic, pine nuts, Parmesan, mayonnaise and yogurt in a food processor or blender and process until smooth. Pour dressing over slaw and toss lightly.

35

V

PINEAPPLE AND KIWI FRUIT SLAW

REALLY EASY!

A salad with an oriental twist – chinese cabbage, red cabbage, pineapple, kiwi fruit and peppers in a pineapple mint dressing.

Serves 6

¼ red cabbage, shredded
½ Chinese cabbage, shredded
400g (14 oz) can pineapple pieces, drained and juice reserved
2 kiwi fruit, peeled and sliced
1 red pepper, seeded and sliced
1 green pepper, seeded and sliced

Dressing

3 tablespoons grapeseed oil
2 tablespoons reserved pineapple juice
3 tablespoons finely chopped fresh coriander
3 tablespoons finely chopped fresh mint

1 Combine red and Chinese cabbages, pineapple, kiwi fruit and red and green peppers in a salad bowl. Toss lightly, cover and refrigerate until required.

2 To make the dressing, combine oil, juice, coriander and mint in a screw-topped jar. Shake well to combine all ingredients, pour over slaw and serve.

MIXED GREEN SALAD

REALLY EASY!

A classic salad that will accompany any dish, hot or cold.

Serves 6

350g (12 oz) mixed lettuce leaves, torn into large pieces
8 spinach leaves, shredded
90g (3 oz) rocket or watercress leaves

Basil Dressing

60 ml (2 fl oz) red wine vinegar
60 ml (2 fl oz) olive oil
2 teaspoons finely grated lime or lemon rind
1 tablespoon chopped fresh basil
1 teaspoon crushed black peppercorns

1 Arrange lettuce leaves, spinach and rocket or watercress in a serving bowl. Cover and chill.

2 To make the dressing, place vinegar, oil, lime or lemon rind, basil and black pepper in a screw-topped jar and shake to combine. Just prior to serving, pour dressing over salad and toss.

GREEK POTATO SALAD

REALLY EASY!

Potatoes tossed in a hot dressing of onions, garlic, vinegar, olives, capers and parsley and then cooled before serving to allow the flavours to mingle.

Serves 6

1 kg (2 lb) potatoes, roughly chopped
2 teaspoons vegetable oil
2 onions, sliced
1 clove garlic, crushed
3 tablespoons white wine vinegar
180g (6 oz) black olives
1 tablespoon capers, drained
2 tablespoons chopped flat-leaf parsley
2 tablespoons olive oil

1 Boil, steam or microwave potatoes until tender. Drain, place in a bowl and set aside to cool.

2 Heat vegetable oil in a frying pan, add onions and garlic and cook over a medium heat, stirring, for 3 minutes or until onions are soft. Add vinegar, olives, capers, parsley and olive oil to pan and mix to combine.

3 Remove pan from heat and set aside to cool. Spoon onion mixture over potatoes and toss gently to combine. Cover and refrigerate until required.

35

V

CHICK-PEA AND PEPPER SALAD

REALLY EASY!

If yellow peppers are unavailable, use another red pepper.

Serves 6-8

2 teaspoons vegetable oil
1 red pepper, seeded and roughly chopped
1 green pepper, seeded and roughly chopped
1 yellow pepper, seeded and roughly chopped
2 cloves garlic, crushed
4 spring onions, sliced diagonally
Two 400g (14 oz) can chick-peas, drained
4 tablespoons pine nuts, toasted

Pine Nut Dressing

4 tablespoons pine nuts, toasted
2 tablespoons olive oil
2 tablespoons lemon juice
3 tablespoons vegetable stock or water
1 tablespoon chopped fresh coriander

1 Heat oil in a large frying pan. Add red, green and yellow peppers, garlic and spring onions and cook over a medium heat, stirring constantly, for 5 minutes or until peppers are soft. Remove pan from heat and set aside to cool.

2 Place chick-peas, pine nuts and pepper mixture in a salad bowl and toss to combine.

3 To make dressing, place pine nuts, oil, lemon juice, stock or water and coriander in a food processor or blender and process until smooth. Spoon dressing over salad, toss to combine, cover and chill until ready to serve.

WATERCRESS AND ORANGE SALAD

REALLY EASY!

A salad of bulgar, watercress, avocado, oranges, tomatoes and red pepper, that goes well with hot or cold poultry.

Serves 6

180g (6 oz) bulgar (cracked wheat)
500 ml (16 fl oz) boiling water
250g (8 oz) watercress, broken into sprigs
1 avocado, stoned, peeled and chopped
2 oranges, peeled,white pith removed, flesh chopped
250g (8 oz) cherry tomatoes, halved
1 red pepper, seeded and diced

Orange Dressing

125 ml (4 fl oz) orange juice
1 tablespoon poppy seeds
2 tablespoons red wine vinegar

1 Place bulgar in a bowl, cover with the boiling water and allow to stand for 10-15 minutes or until soft. Drain well.

2 Place bulgar, watercress, avocado, oranges, tomatoes and red pepper in a salad bowl.

3 To make the dressing, place orange juice, poppy seeds and vinegar in a screw-topped jar and shake well to combine. Spoon dressing over salad and toss to combine. Cover and chill until required.

LENTIL AND MUSHROOM SALAD

V

REALLY EASY!

Lentils with mushroooms, grapes, pepper and pumpkin seeds mixed and marinated in a honey dressing.

Serves 6-8

350g (12 oz) red lentils
250g (8 oz) button mushrooms, halved
4 spring onions, sliced diagonally
4 tablespoons pumpkin seeds
250g (8 oz) seedless grapes
1 yellow or red pepper, seeded and chopped
4 spinach leaves, shredded

Honey Dressing

2 cloves garlic, crushed
1 tablespoon clear honey
2 tablespoons soy sauce
3 tablespoons tarragon vinegar
2 tablespoons vegetable oil
90 ml (3 fl oz) grape juice

1 Bring a large saucepan of water to the boil. Add the lentils, reduce heat and simmer for 30 minutes or until lentils are soft. Drain, rinse under cold running water and drain again.

2 Place lentils, mushrooms, spring onions, pumpkin seeds, grapes, yellow or red pepper and spinach leaves in a large bowl. Toss to combine.

3 To make the dressing, place garlic, honey, soy sauce, vinegar, oil and grape juice in a screw-topped jar and shake well to combine.

4 Spoon dressing over salad, cover and marinate at room temperature for 3 hours before serving.

DESSERTS

Most people still like to have the Traditional Christmas Pudding and a classic recipe is included in this chapter, together with some less traditional, but none the less special ideas for those who wish to serve an alternative.

ICED COINTREAU SOUFFLÉ

EASY!

V

An impressive iced dessert made with eggs, orange, cream and Cointreau.

Serves 10

3 eggs
2 egg yolks
150g (5 oz) caster sugar
grated rind and juice of 1 orange
300 ml (10 fl oz) whipping cream
75 ml (2½ fl oz) Cointreau
orange segments and shredded orange rind to decorate

1 Cut a piece of non-stick baking paper at least 25 cm (10 inch) deep and long enough to wrap around a 600 ml (1 pint) soufflé dish. Fold paper in half lengthways to give a 12 cm (5 inch) band. Wrap this around the dish and secure with a piece of string. The collar should stand about 5 cm (2 inch) above top of dish.

2 Place whole eggs, egg yolks, sugar, orange rind and juice in a large heatproof bowl. Stand bowl over a pan of hot water and whisk continuously using an electric whisk if possible, until mixture forms a thick ribbon when whisk is lifted.

3 Remove bowl from pan and whisk until mixture is cool.

4 Whip cream until it is the same consistency as the whisked mixture, then fold a spoonful of cream into the mixture. Fold in remaining cream and Cointreau. Pour mixture into prepared dish and freeze overnight.

5 To serve, carefully remove paper collar, smooth edge and decorate with orange segments and shredded orange rind.

TRADITIONAL CHRISTMAS PUDDING

EASY!

To light the pudding just before serving, pour about 4 tablespoons warm brandy over the pudding and then ignite with a match.

Makes 2 x 1 kg (2 lb) puddings. Each pudding serves 6-8

180g (6 oz) plain flour
1 tablespoon ground mixed spice
180g (6 oz) shredded suet
125g (4 oz) soft brown sugar
125g (4 oz) fresh white breadcrumbs
grated rind and juice of 1 orange
1 cooking apple
90g (3 oz) glacé cherries, roughly chopped
60g (2 oz) flaked almonds
60g (2 oz) hazelnuts
400g (14 oz) currants
400g (14 oz) raisins
350g (12 oz) sultanas
60g (2 oz) dried dates, chopped
4 eggs, size 3
250 ml (8 fl oz) brown ale
Orange and Brandy Butter to serve, see page 110

1 Grease and line the bases of two 1 kg (2 lb) pudding basins with circles of greaseproof paper.

2 Sieve flour and mixed spice together into a bowl. Add suet, sugar, breadcrumbs and orange rind and juice.

3 Peel, core and grate the cooking apple, then add to bowl with cherries, nuts and fruits.

4 Lightly beat the eggs then add to the fruit mixture with the brown ale. Beat ingredients together until well combined.

5 Divide mixture between prepared basins and level surfaces. Cover with circles of greaseproof paper, securing under rims with string. Cover with foil and secure again with string.

6 Place puddings on upturned saucers in 2 large saucepans. Add 7.5 cm (3 inches) boiling water to pans and cover with lids. Or use a steamer. Steam puddings for 6 hours, topping up with boiling water as necessary. Cool and cover puddings with fresh paper and foil.

7 Reheat as in step 6 for 3 hours. Turn out onto warmed serving plates and serve hot with Orange and Brandy Butter.

EASY CHRISTMAS PUDDING

REALLY EASY!

A quick last-minute pudding if you haven't had time to make the traditional type.

Serves 6

125g (4 oz) butter or margarine
90g (3 oz) soft brown sugar
2 eggs, beaten
180g (6 oz) self-raising flour
1 teaspoon mixed spice
pinch of salt
150g (5 oz) mixed dried fruit
75g (2½ oz) chopped dates
45g (1½ oz) glacé cherries, halved
4 tablespoons sherry or orange juice

1 Grease a 1 litre (32 fl oz) pudding basin. Cream butter or margarine and sugar until light and fluffy. Add the eggs and beat well.

2 Sieve flour with spice and salt. Fold into creamed mixture.

3 Add mixed fruit, dates, cherries and sherry or orange juice and mix well.

4 Spoon mixture into the prepared pudding basin and cover with a tight fitting lid or a double thickness of greaseproof paper or foil. If using paper or foil, tie securely in place with string.

5 Place basin in a saucepan on an upturned plate and add enough boiling water to come half-way up the sides of the pudding basin. Cover saucepan and steam pudding briskly for 2 hours. Add extra boiling water as necessary during cooking to keep the water level at the halfway mark.

6 Turn out the pudding onto a warmed serving plate. Serve with Brandy Cream (page 110) or Pecan and Liqueur Sauce (page 111).

ICED CHRISTMAS PUDDING

V

REALLY EASY!

If you would like a dark pudding, simply use chocolate ice-cream in place of vanilla. Strawberry ice-cream would create a pretty pink pudding.

Serves 10

60g (2 oz) each of sultanas, currants and raisins
125g (4 oz) chopped glacé cherries
60g (2 oz) chopped mixed peel
30g (1 oz) chopped glacé pineapple or stem ginger
60ml (2 fl oz) brandy
1 litre (32 fl oz) vanilla ice-cream
150 ml (5 fl oz) double cream
125g (4 oz) flaked almonds, toasted
60g (2 oz) chocolate chips

1 Mix dried and glacé fruits with brandy. Cover and leave for several hours.

2 Soften ice-cream and place in a bowl with the cream. Stir in fruits, almonds and chocolate chips.

3 Spoon into a 1.75 litre (3 pint) pudding basin and cover with freezer wrap. Freeze overnight.

4 Remove freezer wrap and immerse basin in hot, not boiling, water for 20 seconds. Unmould pudding onto a chilled serving plate and serve.

35

APRICOT SHERRY TRIFLE

REALLY EASY!

V

This trifle is quick to make and easy enough for the kids to give a helping hand.

Serves 6-8

400g (14 oz) packet sponge rolls
125 ml (4 fl oz) sweet sherry, Marsala or port
2 x 400g (14 oz) cans apricot halves, drained
500 ml (16 fl oz) cold prepared custard
142g (4 oz) packet raspberry or strawberry jelly made up according to instructions and set in a shallow tin
300 ml (½ pint) double cream
fresh fruit and chopped nuts to decorate

1 Cut sponge rolls into 1 cm (½ inch) slices and use half the slices to line the base and sides of a glass bowl. Sprinkle slices with half the sherry, Marsala or port.

2 Arrange half the apricots on top of cake and cover with half the custard.

3 Chop jelly into cubes and sprinkle half over the custard. Place another layer of cake slices on top, moisten with remaining sherry, Marsala or port. Add another layer of apricots, custard and jelly.

4 Beat cream until thick and fill a piping bag. Pipe cream in a lattice pattern over top of trifle and decorate with fruit and nuts. Chill until ready to serve.

THE PERFECT PAVLOVA

REALLY EASY!

V

A soft meringue base topped with whipped cream and fresh fruit.

Serves 8

6 egg whites
300g (10 oz) caster sugar
6 teaspoons cornflour, sieved
1½ teaspoons white distilled vinegar
300ml (10 fl oz) double cream, whipped
selection of fresh fruits, such as orange segments, sliced bananas, sliced peaches, seedless grapes, raspberries or sliced kiwi fruit

1 Preheat oven to 120C,250F, Gas ½. Place egg whites in a mixing bowl and whisk until soft peaks form. Gradually add the sugar, beating well after each addition, until mixture is thick and glossy.

2 Fold cornflour and vinegar into egg white mixture. Grease a baking tray and line with non-stick baking paper. Grease paper and dust lightly with flour. Mark a 23 cm (9 inch) diameter circle on paper.

3 Place one-quarter of the egg white mixture in the centre of the circle and spread out to within 3 cm (¼ inch) of the edge. Pile remaining mixture around edge of circle and neaten using a metal spatula or knife. Bake for 1½-2 hours or until firm to touch. Turn off oven and cool pavlova in oven with door ajar. Decorate cold pavlova with cream and top with fruit.

35

V

FRUIT COMPOTE

REALLY EASY!

A simple dessert of peaches poached in red wine and honey.

Serves 4

6 firm ripe peaches, skinned halved and stones removed
250 ml (8 fl oz) red wine
2-3 tablespoons clear honey
1 cinnamon stick

1 Cut peaches into thick slices. Place wine, honey and cinnamon stick into a saucepan and bring to the boil, reduce heat and simmer for 5 minutes. Add peaches and cook for 5-10 minutes or until slightly softened. Set aside to cool, then chill.

MELON SORBET

REALLY EASY!

V

A refreshing water ice made from melon purée – just the thing after a rich meal.

180g (6 oz) caster sugar
300 ml (10 fl oz) water
625 ml (1¼ pint) melon purée
2 egg whites

1 Put the sugar and water in a saucepan and cook over a low heat, stirring, until dissolved. Bring to the boil, reduce the heat and simmer for 10 minutes. Remove from heat and set aside to cool.

2 Mix the melon purée into the sugar syrup, pour into a freezer-proof container and freeze until almost solid.

3 Remove from the freezer and place in a food processor or blender and process until smooth. Beat egg whites until soft peaks form and fold into melon mixture. Return to freezer-proof container and freeze until solid.

CHESTNUT BAVAROIS

A creamy dessert made with chestnut purée, eggs and cream.

Serves 6

7g (¼ oz) powdered gelatine
250 ml (8 fl oz) milk
250g (8 oz) can unsweetened chestnut purée
3 egg yolks
90g (3 oz) caster sugar
470 ml (15 fl oz) whipping cream
whipped cream and 4 marrons glacés to decorate

1 Chill a 900 ml (1½ pint) charlotte tin. Soak gelatine in 1 tablespoon water until spongy. Place milk and half the chestnut purée in a saucepan and bring to the boil mixing well together.

2 Whisk together the egg yolks and 60g (2 oz) of the sugar until thick and light. Stir in a little of the hot milk, then add to the remaining milk in the pan and cook until custard thickens enough to coat back of the spoon. Stir constantly. Do not allow to boil.

3 Add soaked gelatine to hot custard. Cool and then chill until on the point of setting.

4 Whip cream until soft peaks form and set aside. Place remaining chestnut purée in a small bowl and break up with a fork. Add remaining sugar and beat until smooth. Fold in 2 tablespoons of the chilled custard and 1 tablespoon of the cream. Set aside.

5 Fold remaining cream into chilled custard and pour half of this into charlotte tin. Chill until set. Spoon chestnut purée onto the set bavarois and spread evenly with back of spoon. Top with remaining bavarois mixture and chill until completely set.

6 To unmould bavarois, run point of knife around top edge. Dip mould into hot water for a few seconds, then invert onto a chilled plate. Decorate with cream and marrons glacés and serve immediately.

RASPBERRY CHOCOLATE TRUFFLE CAKES

V

A must for all chocolate lovers – light chocolate sponges with a surprise filling of rasperry cream, coated in chocolate and served with chocolate sauce.

Serves 8

60g (2 oz) cocoa powder, sieved
250 ml (8 fl oz) boiling water
125g (4 oz) butter
350g (12 oz) caster sugar
1½ tablespoons raspberry jam
2 eggs
200g (7 oz) self-raising flour, sieved
400g (14 oz) plain chocolate, melted
raspberries for garnishing

Raspberry Cream

125g (4 oz) raspberries, puréed and sieved
125 ml (4 fl oz) double cream, whipped

Chocolate Sauce

125g (4 oz) plain chocolate
125 ml (4 fl oz) water
60g (2 oz) caster sugar
1 teaspoon brandy (optional)

1 Combine cocoa powder and boiling water. Mix to dissolve and set aside to cool. Preheat oven to 180C,350F, Gas 4

2 Place butter, sugar and jam in a bowl and beat until light and fluffy. Beat in eggs one at a time, adding a little flour with each egg. Fold remaining flour and cocoa mixture, alternately, into creamed mixture.

3 Spoon mixture into eight lightly greased 125 ml (4 fl oz) capacity ramekins or large muffin tins. Bake for 20-25 minutes or until cakes are cooked when tested with a skewer. Cool for 5 minutes then turn onto wire racks to cool. Turn cakes upside down and scoop out centre leaving a 1 cm (½ inch) shell. Spread each cake with melted chocolate to cover top and sides, then place right way up on a wire rack. Allow chocolate to set.

4 To make cream, fold raspberry purée into cream. Spoon cream into a piping bag fitted with a large nozzle. Carefully turn cakes upside down and pipe in cream to fill cavity. Place right way up on individual serving plates.

5 To make sauce, place chocolate and water in a small saucepan and cook over a low heat for 4-5 minutes or until melted. Add sugar and continue cooking, stirring constantly, until sugar dissolves.

6 Bring just to the boil, then reduce heat and simmer, stirring, for 2 minutes. Set aside until cool for 5 minutes, then stir in brandy, if using. Cool sauce to room temperature. Pour a little sauce onto each plate around each truffle cake.

BRANDY CREAM

REALLY EASY!

Makes 250ml (8 fl oz)

125 ml (4 fl oz) thick sour cream
125 ml (4 fl oz) double cream
1 tablespoon brown sugar
1 tablespoon brandy

1 To make cream, combine sour cream, cream, brown sugar and brandy in a bowl and mix well.

ORANGE AND BRANDY BUTTER

REALLY EASY!

Serves 6-8

125g (4 oz) unsalted butter, at room temperature
150g (5 oz) icing sugar, sieved
2 teaspoons grated orange rind, optional
1 tablespoon brandy or rum

1 Cream butter until very light and fluffy.

2 Gradually beat in icing sugar and continue beating until mixture is white in colour. Beat in orange rind if using, then brandy or rum. Cover with plastic wrap and store in the refrigerator until required.

35

V

PECAN AND LIQUEUR BUTTER SAUCE

REALLY EASY!

Makes 180g (6 oz)

125g (4 oz) butter, softened
350g (12 oz) icing sugar, sieved
2 tablespoons Baileys Irish Cream
3 tablespoons ground pecan nuts

1 Beat butter until pale and creamy. Add icing sugar a little at a time, beating well after each addition until light and fluffy.

2 Fold in the Irish Cream and nuts.

3 Spoon mixture into a piping bag fitted with a large star piping nozzle. Pipe rosettes onto an oven tray, covered with aluminium foil and freeze until required. Remove from freezer 30 minutes prior to serving.

CAKES

Part of the fun of the Christmas preparations is making the Christmas Cake. On the next few pages are a selection of traditional and novelty cakes plus a couple that would also make lovely gifts.

FESTIVE ALMOND CAKE

REALLY EASY!

V

These little cakes are quick to make and make ideal gifts.

Makes two II x 21 cm (4½ x 8½ inch) cakes

150g (5 oz) glacé apricots, halved
150g (5 oz) red glacé cherries, halved
150g (5 oz) green glacé cherries, halved
90g (3 oz) raisins
125g (4 oz) brazil nuts, chopped
100g (3½ oz) pitted prunes, chopped
125g (4 oz) pecans or walnuts, chopped
100g (3½ oz) ground almonds
½ teaspoon baking powder
3 eggs
2 tablespoons honey
1-2 teaspoons almond essence

1 Preheat oven to 150C,300F, Gas 2. Place apricots, red cherries, green cherries, raisins, brazil nuts, prunes, pecans or walnuts, almonds and baking powder in a bowl and mix to combine.

2 Place eggs in a bowl and beat until thick and creamy. Beat in honey and vanilla essence, then pour egg mixture into fruit mixture and mix to combine.

3 Divide mixture between two greased and lined 11 x 21 cm (4½ x 8½ inch) loaf tins, pressing down firmly, and bake for 1½ hours. Allow cakes to cool in tins.

ROYAL-ICED CHRISTMAS CAKE

V

EASY!

An easy-to-make rich fruit cake very simply iced and decorated with ribbon and purchased decorations of your choice.

Makes a 20 cm (8 inch) round cake

750g (1½ lb) mixed dried fruit
125g (4 oz) glacé cherries, chopped
125g (4 oz) dried apricots, chopped
90g (3 oz) stoned prunes, chopped
60g (2 oz) Brazil nuts, chopped
grated rind and juice of 1 lemon
3 tablespoons brandy
280 g (9 oz) plain flour
2 teaspoons ground mixed spice
200g (7 oz) butter, softened
60g (2 oz) ground almonds
200g (7 oz) soft dark brown sugar
1½ tablespoons black treacle
4 eggs, beaten
750g (1½ lb) white marzipan
3 tablespoons apricot jam, boiled and sieved

Royal Icing

2 egg whites
2 teaspoons glycerine
1½ teaspoons lemon juice
500g (1 lb) icing sugar, sieved
ribbon to trim cake and Christmas cake decorations

1 Line a 20 cm (8 inch) round cake tin with double thickness of greaseproof paper. Preheat oven to 140C,275F, Gas 1.

2 Combine dried fruit, cherries, apricots, prunes, nuts, lemon rind, juice and brandy in a bowl.

3 Mix flour, spice, butter, almonds, sugar, treacle and eggs together in a large bowl, then beat with wooden spoon for 1-2 minutes until smooth and glossy. Stir in fruit mixture.

4 Place mixture in prepared tin, smooth top and bake in oven for 3-3¼ hours, or until a fine skewer inserted into the centre of the cake comes out clean. Cool in tin. When completely cold turn cake out, remove paper and place on a 25 cm (10 inch) round cake board.

5 Roll out marzipan to a 25 cm (10 inch) round. Brush cake with apricot jam, then cover with marzipan. Trim excess marzipan from base of cake.

6 To make royal icing, place egg whites, glycerine and lemon juice in a bowl. Gradually beat in icing sugar until icing peaks softly. Spread icing over cake. Press a palette knife onto icing and pull away sharply to form peaks, leaving a band without peaks around the side, for the ribbon.

7 Tie ribbon around cake and decorate with holly leaves and a selection of Christmas decorations of your choice.

RICH CHRISTMAS CAKE

EASY!

V

Topped with fruit and nuts, this cake makes the perfect alternative to a traditional iced Christmas cake.

Makes a 20 cm (8 inch) round or square cake

250g (8 oz) sultanas
250g (8 oz) currants
250g (8 oz) raisins
125g (4 oz) mixed peel
250g (8 oz) glacé cherries, chopped
60g (2 oz) glacé pineapple, chopped
60g (2 oz) pitted dried dates, chopped
125 ml (4 fl oz) brandy
250g (8 oz) butter, softened
180g (6 oz) brown sugar
5 eggs
60g (2 oz) plain chocolate, melted and cooled
1 teaspoon vanilla essence
1 teaspoon almond essence
2 teaspoons glycerine
2 tablespoons raspberry jam
1 teaspoon finely grated lemon rind
2 tablespoons lemon juice
250g (8 oz) flour
1 teaspoon ground mixed spice
1 teaspoon ground ginger
¼ teaspoon salt

Fruit And Nut Topping

2 tablespoons apricot jam
90g (3 oz) pecan or walnut halves
90g (3 oz) brazil nuts
60g (2 oz) blanched almonds
60g (2 oz) red glacé cherries
60g (2 oz) green glacé cherries

1 Place sultanas, currants, raisins, mixed peel, chopped cherries, pineapple and dates in a bowl. Pour over 4 tablespoons brandy and toss to combine. Cover and stand overnight.

2 Preheat the oven to 150C,300F, Gas 2. Lightly grease a 20 cm (8 inch) round or square cake tin and line base and sides of tin with double thickness non-stick baking or greaseproof paper.

3 Place butter in a large bowl and beat until light and fluffy. Gradually add brown sugar, beating well after each addition. Add eggs one at a time, beating well after each addition. Stir in chocolate, vanilla essence, almond essence, glycerine, jam, lemon rind and lemon juice.

4 Sieve together flour, mixed spice, ginger and salt. Stir flour mixture and fruit mixture, alternately, into butter mixture and mix well to combine.

5 Spoon batter into prepared tin and smooth top. Drop tin onto a flat surface to break up any air bubbles and cook in the oven for 3-3½ hours or until cooked when tested with a skewer. Remove cake from oven, sprinkle with remaining brandy and set aside to cool in tin. When completely cold remove cake from tin. If you are planning to store the cake, leave the paper on, wrap cake in a double thickness of foil and store in an airtight container.

6 To decorate, place jam in a small saucepan and heat, stirring over a low heat until melted, then push through a sieve. Brush top of cake with warm jam and then arrange pecans or walnuts, brazil nuts, almonds and cherries in an attractive pattern on the top.

BUCHE DE NOEL

V **Despite its delicate texture and creamy frosting, this cake may be frozen up to 3 weeks ahead of serving.**

Serves 10-12

Sponge

60g (2 oz) plain flour
½ teaspoon baking powder
¼ teaspoon salt
60g (2 oz) plain chocolate, chopped
4 eggs
180g (6 oz) caster sugar
1 teaspoon vanilla essence
2 tablespoons warm water
¼ teaspoon bicarbonate of soda
icing sugar

Buttercream

180g (6 oz) butter, softened
500g (1 lb) icing sugar
4 tablespoons cocoa powder
2-3 tablespoons milk

1 Lightly grease a 30 x 25 cm (12 x 10 inch) Swiss roll tin. Cut a rectangle of greaseproof paper or non-stick baking paper about 3 cm (1½ inch) wider all around than the tin. Cut slits 2 cm (¾ inch) long in each corner of the paper. Fit into the tin, tucking corners under so they fit neatly. If using greaseproof paper, grease lightly.

2 Preheat oven to 200C,400F, Gas 6. Sieve flour, baking powder and salt onto a sheet of greaseproof paper and set aside. Place chocolate in a bowl set over a saucepan of simmering water and stir until melted. Set aside. Place eggs and sugar in a large mixing bowl and beat at high speed with an electric mixer for about 5 minutes, until thick and light. The mixture should be thick enough to leave a trail when beaters are lifted.

3 Add the sieved flour and vanilla essence all at once and fold in gently and quickly with a metal spoon. Add water and bicarbonate of soda to melted chocolate and stir until thick and smooth. Pour chocolate into egg and flour mixture. Fold in with a metal spoon until ingredients are just combined. Do not beat mixture.

4 Pour mixture into the prepared tin and shake gently so it reaches into the corners. Bake in oven for 15 minutes, or until cake springs back when lightly touched with fingers. Remove cake from oven and turn out onto a clean tea-towel which has been sprinkled thickly with icing sugar.

5 Peel off the lining paper and trim off the crisp edges of cake with a sharp knife.

6 Fold the hem of the tea-towel over the short edge of the cake and roll up cake, using the tea-towel to help roll. Place roll on a wire rack and leave until completely cold.

7 For the buttercream, beat butter until soft and light. Sieve icing sugar and cocoa into butter. Beat until mixture is smooth and creamy. Add milk and beat until combined. Carefully unroll the cake and spread quickly with half the buttercream. Roll up again.

8 Cut two 1 cm (½ inch) slices on the slant from the cake and arrange on top to resemble a gnarled log. Frost entire cake with remaining buttercream and use a fork to make whorls and lines resembling bark. Chill cake until ready to serve and decorate with a sprig of holly.

CHOCOLATE CHRISTMAS PUDDING CAKE

V

EASY!

This delightful chocolate cake makes a lovely change from traditional rich fruit cake for Christmas. It makes a perfect centrepiece for a party buffet table and can be decorated up to 2 days in advance and kept in a cool place.

Serves 8-10

6 eggs, size 2
150g (5 oz) butter
180g (6 oz) caster sugar
125g (4 oz) plain chocolate
150g (5 oz) plain flour
1 teaspoon baking powder

Icing

250g (8 oz) chocolate buttercream made with 90g (3 oz) butter and 180g (6 oz) icing sugar
250g (8 oz) plain chocolate
90 ml (3 fl oz) double cream
handful of small raisins or currants
90g (3 oz) sugarpaste (fondant icing)

1 Grease and flour two halves of a 20 cm (8 inch) diameter spherical cake mould or two 625 ml (20 fl oz) pudding basins. Preheat oven to 180C,350F, Gas 4.

2 Separate the eggs. Place butter and 125g (4 oz) of the sugar in a bowl and cream together. Beat in egg yolks, one at a time.

3 Break up the chocolate, place in a heatproof bowl and melt over a saucepan of hot water. Alternatively, melt chocolate in a microwave-proof bowl in microwave on full power for about 1 minute. Add chocolate to sugar and egg mixture.

4 Whisk egg whites until light and fluffy, then fold in remaining sugar. Sieve flour and baking powder together, then carefully fold into chocolate mixture alternating spoonfuls of flour and meringue.

5 Pour cake mixture into mould or pudding basins. Bake in two separate halves for about 30 minutes until firm to the touch.

6 Allow cakes to cool, then turn out and trim flat surfaces level. Spread halves with buttercream then join together. If using basins, trim to a round shape with a sharp serrated knife. Cover cake all over with a thin layer of buttercream. Put cake in refrigerator and allow to set for 30 minutes.

7 Meanwhile, melt the chocolate as in step 3. In a small saucepan, bring cream to boiling point, then stir into melted chocolate. Place cake on a cooling rack over a baking tray or similar, to catch the drips, and spread chocolate mixture over the cake scooping up excess as necessary and making sure all the cake is covered. Press a few raisins or currants into chocolate before it sets. Transfer cake to a cake board.

8 Roll out sugarpaste on a surface lightly dusted with icing sugar, keeping back a small amount for holly. Cut 'poured cream shape' out of sugarpaste and press onto top of cake. Colour most of the remaining sugarpaste green and a small amount red. Roll out and cut out holly leaves out of the green sugarpaste using a cutter or sharp knife and roll small pieces of red sugarpaste with fingers to form berries. Stick leaves and berries to top of 'cream' with a little water.

CHRISTMAS STOLLEN

EASY!

V **Stollen make wonderful gifts for friends and they look very inviting wrapped in clear cellophane and tied with red and green ribbons.**

Makes 2 Stollen. Serves 12

350g (12 oz) mixed dried fruit
90g (3 oz) blanched almonds, chopped
2 tablespoons dark rum
30g (1 oz) fresh yeast
60 ml (2 fl oz) lukewarm water
125g (4 oz) caster sugar
600g (1¼ lb) plain flour
250 ml (8 fl oz) lukewarm milk
2 eggs, beaten
250g (8 oz) butter, cut into small pieces and softened
½ teaspoon salt
30g (1 oz) butter, melted
beaten egg for glaze
sieved icing sugar or glacé icing to decorate

1 Combine the dried fruit, almonds and rum. Crumble yeast into a small bowl. Stir in lukewarm water and 1 teaspoon of the sugar. Stir until yeast dissolves. Set aside for 5 minutes until frothy.

2 Sieve 250g (8 oz) flour into a large bowl. Stir in the yeast mixture and lukewarm milk. Cover with plastic wrap and let stand in a warm place for about 1 hour until dough has doubled in volume. Preheat oven to 190C,375F, Gas 5.

3 Knock down the dough flrmly with your flst and work in the beaten eggs, remaining caster sugar and pieces of softened butter.

4 Sieve remaining 350g (12 oz) flour with salt and work

250g (8 oz) into the dough to form a soft mixture. This is easiest to do by hand. Turn dough out onto a lightly floured surface and knead in enough of remaining flour to form a smooth and satiny dough without any stickiness. Work in fruit and nut mixture.

5 Divide dough in half. On a lightly floured surface, pat or roll each portion into an oval shape about 30 x 20 cm (12 x 8 inch) and 2 cm (¾ inch) thick. Put on a baking tray. Brush each piece with melted butter and fold the dough over lengthwise, almost in half.

6 Lightly press edges together to seal and brush tops with beaten egg. Bake in oven for 35-40 minutes until well risen and golden brown. Remove from oven and brush tops again with melted butter. When cool, dust the Stollen generously with sieved icing sugar or drizzle with glacé icing (see page 124) and decorate with glacé fruits and nuts.

GLACÉ ICING

V

180g (6 oz) icing sugar, sieved
2-3 teaspoons warm water, or orange or lemon juice

1 Place icing sugar in a bowl and gradually add enough water, or orange or lemon juice until icing is of a consistency to coat the back of a spoon.

2 Pour icing over stollen and decorate with fruits and nuts while icing is still soft. Allow icing to set before slicing.

CHERRY MADEIRA CAKE

EASY!

V

This cake will keep well, wrapped in foil and stored in an air-tight container, for up to 2 weeks.

Serves 12

180g (6 oz) butter, softened
180g (6 oz) caster sugar
3 eggs, beaten
180g (6 oz) self-raising flour, sieved
60g (2 oz) ground almonds
150g (5 oz) glacé cherries, finely chopped

To Glaze

2 tablespoons apricot jam, boiled and sieved
60g (2 oz) glacé cherries, halved
3 glacé pineapple rings, cut into pieces

1 Lightly grease and line an 18 cm (7 inch) round cake tin. Preheat oven to 170C,325F, Gas 3.

2 Beat butter and sugar together in a bowl until light and fluffy. Gradually add the eggs, beating well after each addition. Add the flour, ground almonds, chopped cherries and fold carefully into mixture.

3 Place mixture into prepared tin, smooth top and bake for 1-1¼ hours or until cake springs back when pressed in the centre. Cool in tin 5 minutes, turn out onto a wire rack. Remove paper, invert cake and leave until cold.

4 Brush apricot glaze over top of cake. Arrange halved glacé cherries and pineapple pieces on top and brush with remaining glaze.

WHITE CHRISTMAS CAKE

EASY!

To prevent dried fruit from sinking to the bottom of a cake, toss the fruit in a tablespoon of the flour used in the recipe before adding to the cake batter.

Makes a 20 cm (8 inch) round cake

180g (6 oz) sultanas
200g (7 oz) glacé cherries, halved
1 tablespoon finely grated lemon rind
180 ml (6 fl oz) brandy
180g (6 oz) butter
180g (6 oz) sugar
4 eggs, separated
300g (10 oz) plain flour
1 teaspoon baking powder
1 teaspoon ground mixed spice
½ teaspoon ground cinnamon
60g (2 oz) blanched almonds

1 Place sultanas, 180g (6 oz) cherries and lemon rind in a bowl, pour over 125 ml (4 fl oz) brandy and mix to combine. Cover and set aside to stand overnight.

2 Preheat oven to 180C,350F, Gas 4. Place butter in a bowl and beat until light and fluffy. Gradually add sugar, beating well after each addition. Add egg yolks one at a time, beating well after each addition.

3 Sieve together flour, baking powder, mixed spice and cinnamon. Fold flour mixture and fruit mixture, alternately, into butter mixture.

4 Place egg whites in a clean bowl and whisk until soft peaks form. Fold egg white mixture into fruit mixture. Spoon batter into a greased and lined 20 cm (8 inch) round cake tin and smooth top with a spatula. Arrange almonds and remaining cherries decoratively on top of cake and bake for 1½ hours or until cooked when tested with a skewer. Using skewer, pierce the cake several times then sprinkle with remaining brandy. Wrap cake in a tea-towel and set aside to cool completely before turning out.

DUNDEE CAKE

EASY!

V

A moist fruit cake with a topping of whole almonds.

Makes a 20 cm (8 inch) round cake

250g (8 oz) butter, softened
1 teaspoon rum essence
200g (7 oz) caster sugar
4 eggs, lightly beaten
250g (8 oz) flour
1 teaspoon baking powder
3 tablespoons cornflour
250g (8 oz) sultanas
250g (8 oz) currants
125g (4 oz) mixed peel
125g (4 oz) slivered almonds
60g (2 oz) glacé cherries, halved
2 teaspoons finely grated orange rind
1 tablespoon orange juice
45g (1½ oz) blanched almonds

1 Preheat oven to 150C,300F, Gas 2. Place butter and rum essence in a bowl and beat until light and fluffy. Gradually add sugar, beating well after each addition until mixture is creamy.

2 Add eggs one at a time, beating well after each addition. Sieve together flour, baking powder and cornflour and fold into the butter mixture.

3 Stir in sultanas, currants, mixed peel, slivered almonds, cherries, orange rind and orange juice. Spoon mixture into a greased and lined deep 20 cm (8 inch) cake tin. Decorate top of cake with almonds, arranged in circles, and bake for 2½-3 hours, or until cooked when tested with a skewer. Set aside to cool in tin before turning out.

GINGERBREAD CAKE

REALLY EASY!

V

A spicy ginger cake cooked in a ring tin and glazed with a tangy lemon icing.

Makes a 20 cm (8 inch) ring cake

125g (4 oz) butter, melted
125 ml (4 fl oz) hot water
180g (6 oz) golden syrup, warmed
125g (4 oz) plain flour, sieved
60g (2 oz) self-raising flour, sieved
½ teaspoon bicarbonate of soda
4 teaspoons ground ginger
½ teaspoon ground nutmeg
90g (3 oz) brown sugar

Lemon Icing

200g (7 oz) icing sugar, sieved
15g (½ oz) butter, softened
1 tablespoon lemon juice
milk

1 Preheat oven to 180C,350F, Gas 4. Place butter, water and golden syrup in a large bowl. Sieve in plain flour, self-raising flour, bicarbonate of soda, ginger, nutmeg and sugar and mix to combine all ingredients.

2 Spoon batter into a greased 20 cm (8 inch) ring cake tin and bake for 35-40 minutes or until cake is cooked when tested with a skewer. Leave cake in tin for 5 minutes before turning onto a wire rack to cool.

3 To make icing, place icing sugar in a bowl, mix in butter, lemon juice and enough milk to make an icing of spreading consistency. Spread icing over cold cake with a palette knife.

TEA TIME TREATS

Home-made biscuits and little sweet treats are easy to make and are always appreciated. It's nice to have some treats on hand for last minute gifts and for those unexpected visitors who pop in over Christmas.

CHOCOLATE TRUFFLES

REALLY EASY!

V **If preferred, roll the truffles in finely grated white or plain chocolate, toasted coconut or finely chopped mixed nuts.**

Makes about 25 truffles

250g (8 oz) plain chocolate, broken into pieces
1½ tablespoons instant coffee powder
3 tablespoons hot water
125g (4 oz) unsalted butter, cut into small pieces and left at room temperature
3 tablespoons coffee or chocolate flavoured liqueur
about 60g (2 oz) cocoa powder
25 small paper cases

1 Place chocolate, coffee powder and hot water in a heatproof bowl over a pan of simmering water. Stir until chocolate melts then remove bowl from heat.

2 Using a wire whisk, beat butter into chocolate mixture a piece at a time. When all the butter is incorporated, beat in liqueur. Cover bowl and chill mixture until firm.

3 Sieve cocoa onto a sheet of greaseproof paper. Using a teaspoon, take out walnut-sized pieces of mixture and shape them into balls.

4 Roll the balls in cocoa, then transfer to paper cases. Refrigerate until ready to serve.

MINCE PIES

EASY!

Add interest to the pies by decorating in various ways. Use biscuit cutters to cut out star, holly leaf or angel shapes; or lattice strips of pastry over the mincemeat. For plain lids, make a small hole in the top of the pie to allow steam to escape during cooking.

Makes 12 pies

Mincemeat

125g (4 oz) each currants, sultanas and raisins
125g (4 oz) chopped mixed peel
125g (4 oz) shredded suet
90g (3 oz) almonds, chopped
1 large Granny Smith apple, peeled, cored and grated
juice and grated rind of 2 lemons
juice and grated rind of 1 large orange
227g (8 oz) can crushed pineapple, drained, optional
60g (2 oz) soft brown sugar
1 teaspoon mixed spice
60 ml (2 fl oz) brandy

Pastry

125g (4 oz) butter
125g (4 oz) caster sugar
1 egg
125g (4 oz) self-raising flour
125g (4 oz) plain flour
1 egg white, lightly beaten

1 To make the mincemeat, combine all ingredients well together. Spoon into jars with tight-fltting lids and store in the refrigerator until required. The flavour of fruit mince develops and grows richer with time, so try to store for at least a week before baking pies.

2 For the pastry, cream together the butter and sugar. Add egg and beat in. Sieve flours together and fold in. Knead lightly, wrap in plastic wrap and chill for 1 hour. Preheat oven to 180C,350F, Gas 4. Roll dough out on a floured surface and cut out twelve 7.5 cm (3 inch) rounds with a fluted pastry cutter.

3 Fit rounds into well-greased or non-stick tartlet cases or patty tins. Spoon filling into cases. From remaining pastry, cut out the lids. Brush lids with egg white and bake pies in oven for 25 minutes, or until pastry is golden. Cool in the tins for a minute before removing to wire racks to cool.

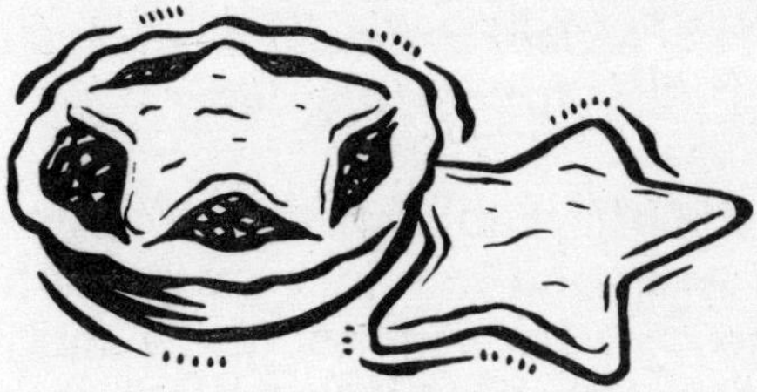

CRUNCHY CHOCOLATE SLICE

REALLY EASY!

Easy enough for children to make and so delicious you may wish to make double the quantity.

Serves 8

60g (2 oz) butter
500g (1 lb) plain chocolate
75 ml (2½ fl oz) strong black coffee
1 tablespoon golden syrup
1 tablespoon rum
250g (8 oz) shortbread or digestive biscuits
125g (4 oz) dates, stoned and chopped
125g (4 oz) glacé cherries, halved
1 banana, roughly chopped
125g (4 oz) chopped mixed nuts

To Decorate

6 glacé cherries, halved
strips of angelica

1 Grease a 750g (1½ lb) loaf tin. Place butter, chocolate, coffee, syrup and rum in a heatproof bowl over a pan of simmering water and heat gently until chocolate is melted. Remove from heat and stir until smooth.

2 Roughly break up half the shortbread (or digestives). Crush remaining biscuits.

3 Add dates, cherries, banana, nuts and both the crushed and roughly broken shortbread (or digestives) to the chocolate mixture and stir well. Spoon into prepared tin and level top. Cover and chill overnight.

4 To serve, run the point of a small knife around sides of the tin and invert onto a serving plate. Decorate top with cherries and angelica. Cut into thin slices to serve.

35

GINGER CRUNCH

REALLY EASY!

V

Crushed ginger nut biscuits mixed with butter, sugar, condensed milk, walnuts and ginger.

Makes 30

125g (4 oz) butter
180g (6 oz) caster sugar
I25 ml (4 fl oz) sweetened condensed milk
1 tablespoon golden syrup
250g (8 oz) gingernut biscuits, crushed
60g (2 oz) pecans or walnuts, finely chopped
2 tablespoons finely chopped glacé ginger or stem ginger in syrup, drained and chopped

1 Place butter, sugar, condensed milk and golden syrup in a small saucepan and cook over a medium heat, stirring constantly, until mixture is smooth. Bring to the boil, then reduce heat and simmer for 3-4 minutes or until mixture thickens slightly.

2 Place biscuits, pecans or walnuts and glacé or stem ginger in a bowl, pour in condensed milk mixture and mix until well combined. Press mixture into a lined, shallow 23 cm (9 inch) square cake tin and refrigerate until set. Cut into bars.

CHRISTMAS TREE BISCUITS

REALLY EASY!

V

Lovely to make to hang on the Christmas tree. Children will love to help cut out and decorate these spicy biscuits.

Makes about 40 biscuits

350g (12 oz) plain flour
2 teaspoons baking powder
2 teaspoons ground cinnamon
1 teaspoon ground mixed spice
1 teaspoon ground ginger
¼ teaspoon salt
250g (8 oz) butter, softened
180g (6 oz) soft brown sugar
3 tablespoons brandy, rum or orange juice
1 egg white, lightly beaten
sultanas, raisins, almonds and glacé cherries to decorate

1 Preheat oven to 180C,350F, Gas 4. Sieve together flour, baking powder, cinnamon, spice, ginger and salt and set aside. Cream butter with an electric mixer or wooden spoon and gradually beat in sugar. Add brandy, rum or orange juice, then dry ingredients. Stir until well combined and a soft dough is formed. Wrap in plastic wrap and chill for 30 minutes.

2 Turn out dough onto a lightly floured surface and roll out with a floured rolling pin to make a rectangle about 5 mm (¼ inch) thick. Cut dough into shapes with decorative biscuit cutters.

3 Arrange biscuits on greased baking trays and brush with egg white. Use a metal skewer to mark patterns on each biscuit and decorate with sultanas, raisins, almonds and cherries. Make a hole in the top of each for threading ribbon. Bake in oven for 15 minutes or until firm to touch. Transfer biscuits onto a wire rack to cool.

4 Store biscuits in an airtight container. To decorate, thread ribbon through holes in biscuits and tie to the branches of the Christmas tree.

ORANGE SHORTBREAD

REALLY EASY!

V

Shortbread is always associated with Christmas so try this recipe which has an unexpected orange flavour.

Makes 20 squares

250g (8 oz) butter
125g (4 oz) caster sugar plus 1 tablespoon
3 teaspoons orange juice
1 teaspoon finely grated orange rind
250g (8 oz) plain flour
60g (2 oz) cornflour

1 Preheat oven to 180C,350F, Gas 4. Place butter and 125g (4 oz) sugar in a bowl and beat until light and fluffy. Beat in orange juice and orange rind. Sieve together flour and cornflour and fold into butter mixture.

2 Press mixture into a greased and lined 20 cm (8 inch) square cake tin. Mark into squares, prick with a fork, sprinkle with remaining caster sugar and bake for 30-40 minutes or until just golden. Allow to cool in tin, then cut into squares.

CHRISTMAS COOKIES

REALLY EASY!

V

Crisp liitle biscuits with added hazelnuts, chocolate chips, coconut, sultanas and cherries.

Makes 25

125g (4 oz) butter
200g (7 oz) caster sugar
1 egg, lightly beaten
2 teaspoons vanilla essence
60 ml (2 fl oz) milk
150g (5 oz) plain flour
½ teaspoon bicarbonate of soda
90g (3 oz) roasted hazelnuts, chopped
125g (4 oz) chocolate chips
90g (3 oz) shredded coconut
90g (3 oz) sultanas
90g (3 oz) glacé cherries, chopped

1 Preheat oven to 180C,350F, Gas 4. Place butter and sugar in a bowl and beat until light and fluffy. Beat in egg, vanilla essence and milk and continue to beat until well combined.

2 Stir together flour and bicarbonate of soda and stir into butter mixture. Add hazelnuts, chocolate chips, coconut, sultanas and cherries and mix until well combined.

3 Drop tablespoons of mixture onto greased baking trays and bake for 15 minutes or until golden. Remove to wire racks to cool completely.

CARAMEL SQUARES

EASY!

V **These rich little squares have a shortbread base, creamy caramel filling and a layer of plain chocolate on top.**

Makes 25

Shortbread Base

100g (3½ oz) butter
3 tablespoons caster sugar
60g (2 oz) cornflour, sieved
90g (3 oz) flour, sieved

Caramel Filling

125g (4 oz) butter
90g (3 oz) brown sugar
2 tablespoons honey
400g (14 oz) can sweetened condensed milk
1 teaspoon vanilla essence

Chocolate Topping

200g (7 oz) plain chocolate, melted

1 Preheat oven to 180C,350F, Gas 4.

2 To make base, place butter and sugar in a bowl and beat until light and fluffy. Mix in cornflour and flour, turn onto a lightly floured surface and knead briefly, then press into a greased and lined 18 x 28 cm (7 x 11 inch) shallow cake tin and bake for 25 minutes or until firm.

3 To make filling, place butter, brown sugar and honey in a saucepan and cook over a medium heat, stirring constantly until sugar melts and ingredients are combined. Bring to the boil and simmer for 7 minutes. Beat in condensed milk and vanilla essence, pour filling over base and bake for 20 minutes longer. Set aside to cool completely.

4 Spread melted chocolate over filling, set aside until firm, then cut into squares.

FRUIT SHORTCAKE

REALLY EASY!

V

This can be served in wedges for tea and it also makes a tasty pudding served with cream or custard.

Serves 8

250g (8 oz) self-raising flour, sieved
125g (4 oz) butter
100g (3½ oz) caster sugar, plus 2 tablespoons
1 egg, beaten
1 tablespoon lemon juice
200g (7 oz) prepared mincemeat
1 egg white, lightly beaten

1 Preheat oven to 180C,350F, Gas 4. Place flour, butter and 100g (3½ oz) sugar in a food processor and process until mixture resembles fine breadcrumbs. With machine running, slowly add egg and enough lemon juice to make a firm dough. Turn onto a floured surface and knead briefly. Wrap dough in plastic food wrap and refrigerate for 30 minutes.

2 Divide dough in half. Roll out one half large enough to cover the base and sides of a greased 20 cm (8 inch) sandwich tin. Spread mincemeat over base.

3 Roll out remaining dough large enough to cover mincemeat. Press edges together firmly. Brush with egg white and sprinkle with remaining sugar. Bake for 30-35 minutes or until cooked. Stand for 10 minutes before turning onto a wire rack to cool completely. Cut into wedges to serve.

DISHES WITH LEFTOVERS

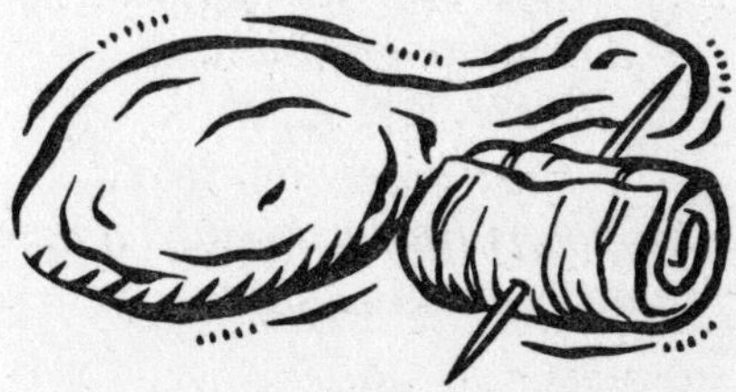

It is not only turkey that is left over after Christmas, but often cooked gammon or ham and cheese as well. On the next few pages are some tempting ideas for using cooked turkey, chicken, gammon and cheese. These recipes will help you use up all those little bits and pieces left in the fridge and transform them into delicious new dishes.

TURKEY AND CHUTNEY LOAF

REALLY EASY!

If preferred, replace the cooked turkey with an equal quantity of cooked lean ham. This loaf is delicious served hot with a spicy tomato sauce.

Serves 6

350g (12 oz) cooked turkey, finely chopped
90g (3 oz) fresh white breadcrumbs
2 eggs
1 small onion, chopped
2 tablespoons chutney
90 ml (3 fl oz) milk
2-3 teaspoons paprika
4 tablespoons finely chopped parsley
cherry tomatoes and salad leaves to serve

1 Preheat oven to 180C,350F, Gas 4. Place all ingredients in a large bowl and mix well.

2 Press mixture into a greased and base lined 500g (1 lb) loaf tin and bake in the oven for 35-40 minutes. Serve loaf sliced, hot or cold with tomatoes and salad.

35

CREAMY TURKEY SOUP

REALLY EASY!

Using cooked turkey or chicken is a quick and easy way to make soup, but remember, do not cook the turkey or chicken for too long after adding to the soup or it will end up as unpalatable strings.

Serves 8

15g (½ oz) butter
1 clove garlic, finely chopped
2 litres (3½ pints) turkey or chicken stock
1 kg (2 lb) cooked turkey or chicken, finely chopped
2 teaspoons Worcestershire sauce
500 ml (16 fl oz) double cream
freshly ground black pepper
3-4 tablespoons chopped fresh parsley
3-4 tablespoons snipped fresh chives

1 Melt butter in a large saucepan and cook garlic over a low heat for 2-3 minutes. Add stock, bring to the boil, then reduce heat to simmering. Stir in turkey or chicken and Worcestershire sauce and cook for 2-3 minutes.

2 Stir in cream and season to taste with black pepper. Add parsley and chives and cook over a medium heat for 4-5 minutes or until soup is hot.

TURKEY AND STILTON OPEN SANDWICHES

REALLY EASY!

You can use any blue cheese for this recipe or you might like to use Brie or Camembert or a cream cheese instead.

Serves 6

1 French stick, cut into 12 thick slices
2 tablespoons Dijon mustard
12 slices cooked turkey
200g (7 oz) Stilton cheese, crumbled
30g (1 oz) watercress, broken into sprigs

1 Spread each slice of bread with mustard. Top with turkey and cheese and garnish with watercress. Serve immediately.

TURKEY AND CHEESE MUFFINS

REALLY EASY!

A delicious little snack to keep away hunger pangs, or to eat when you fancy a nibble but are too full to have a whole meal.

Serves 2

2 muffins, split and toasted
1 tomato, sliced
4 thin slices cooked turkey breast
3 tablespoons grated cheese
freshly ground black pepper

1 Top each muffin half with tomato slices, turkey, cheese and black pepper to taste and cook under a preheated grill for 2-3 minutes or until cheese melts.

TURKEY AND THREE RICE SALAD

REALLY EASY!

Wild rice is the grain from an aquatic grass which grows in North America. It has a pleasant nutty flavour and takes 30-45 minutes to cook. The grains should burst when they are cooked.

Serves 6

1 litre (1¾ pints) chicken stock
60g (2 oz) wild rice
60g (2 oz) brown rice
60g (2 oz) white rice
1 large spinach leaf, finely shredded
125g (4 oz) button mushrooms, sliced
4 spring onions, chopped
1 red pepper, seeded and cut into strips
2 tablespoons pine nuts, toasted
750g (1½ lb) cooked, sliced turkey or chicken cut in strips

Curried Coconut Dressing

125 ml (4 fl oz) coconut milk
1 teaspoon grated fresh root ginger
2 tablespoons white wine vinegar
2 teaspoons brown sugar
½ teaspoon curry powder
¼ teaspoon ground turmeric
freshly ground black pepper

1 Place stock in a large saucepan and bring to the boil. Add wild and brown rice and cook for 25 minutes. Add white rice and cook for 15 minutes longer or until all the grains are tender. Drain and rinse under cold running water.

2 Place drained rice, spinach, mushrooms, spring onions, red pepper, pine nuts and turkey in a bowl and toss to combine.

3 To make dressing, place coconut milk, ginger, vinegar, sugar, curry powder, turmeric and black pepper to taste in a screw-topped jar and shake well to combine. Spoon dressing over salad and serve immediately.

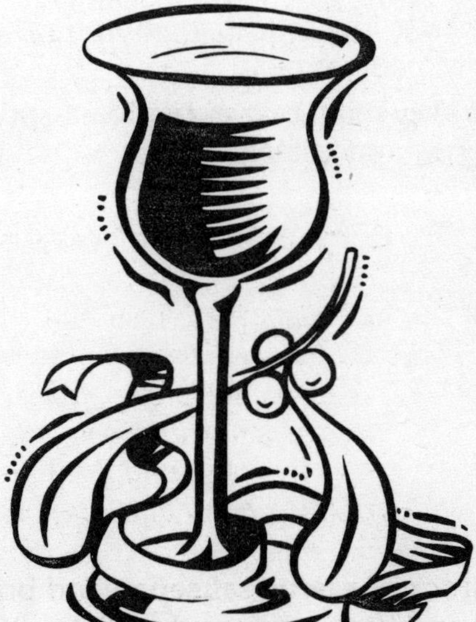

TURKEY HASH

REALLY EASY!

If you do not have leftover gravy for this dish, use a can of cream of mushroom soup instead.

Serves 4

350g (12 oz) cooked turkey, chopped
2 potatoes, cooked and diced
250 ml (8 fl oz) leftover turkey gravy
2 spring onions, chopped
freshly ground black pepper
4 slices wholegrain bread, toasted and lightly buttered
2 tablespoons chopped fresh parsley

1 Place turkey, potatoes, gravy, spring onions and black pepper to taste in a saucepan and bring to the boil, stirring, over a medium heat.

2 Spoon turkey mixture over hot toast, sprinkle with parsley and serve immediately.

35

TURKEY CREOLE

REALLY EASY!

Serve this dish on a bed of cooked rice.

Serves 4

15g (½ oz) butter
1 clove garlic, crushed
1 onion, chopped
1 tablespoon plain flour
1 teaspoon chilli powder
125 ml (4 fl oz) tomato juice
125 ml (4 fl oz) chicken or turkey stock
350g (12 oz) cooked turkey, chopped
125g (4 oz) button mushrooms, sliced
freshly ground black pepper

1 Heat the butter in a saucepan and cook the garlic and onion over a medium heat for 3-4 minutes or until the onion is soft. Stir in the flour and chilli powder and cook, stirring for 1 minute.

2 Stir in the tomato juice and stock. Bring to the boil, stirring, over a medium heat, then reduce the heat and simmer, stirring, until the sauce thickens. Add the turkey and mushrooms, season to taste with black pepper and bring to the boil. Reduce the heat and simmer for 5 minutes until heated through.

HAM AND MUSHROOM ROLLS

REALLY EASY!

You can vary this recipe as you please. Ham slices can be replaced with turkey, the cream cheese can be replaced with mashed Danish blue or Stilton and celery or tomato soup can be used instead of mushroom.

Serves 4

8 large slices ham
180g (6 oz) cream cheese
180 ml (6 fl oz) sour cream
1 egg, lightly beaten
1 small onion, finely chopped
125g (4 oz) cooked spinach, well drained and chopped
pinch each of nutmeg and powder mustard
salt and pepper to taste
celery leaves to garnish

Mushroom Sauce

250 ml (8 fl oz) cream of mushroom soup
60 ml (2 fl oz) sour cream

1 Preheat oven to 180C,350F, Gas 4. Remove any fat from ham. Combine cheese, sour cream, egg, onion, spinach and seasonings. Place about 2 tablespoons of filling on each slice of ham and roll up.

2 Arrange rolls seam-side down in a shallow baking dish. Combine sauce ingredients and salt and pepper, then spoon over rolls. Bake in oven for 25 minutes. Garnish with celery leaves.

HAM AND POTATO CAKES

REALLY EASY!

Quickly made and cooked these savoury cakes are just the thing for the kids' tea.

Serves 4

180g (6 oz) ham, finely chopped
1 medium potato, cooked and mashed
1 tablespoon snipped chives or 2 spring onions, chopped
freshly ground black pepper to taste
60g (2 oz) plain flour
2 tablespoons vegetable oil
4 slices fresh or canned pineapple
salad leaves to serve

1 Combine ham, potato, chives or spring onions and pepper.

2 Shape mixture into 4 cakes and coat them lightly in flour. Heat oil in a frying pan and fry cakes on both sides until golden brown, allowing about 3 minutes each side.

3 Drain ham cakes. Serve with pineapple and salad.

THREE CHEESE PIZZA

EASY!

Pizza dough topped with onions, tomatoes, herbs and a wonderful mixture of three cheeses – tasty Stilton, creamy mozzarella and vibrant red Leicester.

Serves 6

Pizza Dough

15g (½ oz) dried yeast
125 ml (4 fl oz) warm water
500g (1 lb) plain flour
good pinch of salt
2 tablespoons olive oil

Topping

45g (1½ oz) butter
2 large onions, sliced
3 tomatoes, skinned and chopped
2 tablespoons chopped fresh basil or marjoram
125g (4 oz) blue Stilton cheese, crumbled
125g (4 oz) mozzarella cheese, sliced
125g (4 oz) red Leicester or Cheddar cheese, grated

1 To prepare dough, dissolve the yeast in the water in a cup. Sieve the flour and salt into a bowl, then stir in the oil and yeast liquid, adding a little extra water if necessary to give a smooth dough. Knead well, then divide in half and roll into two 20 cm (8 inch) circles. Place on oiled baking sheets, cover loosely with plastic wrap and leave to rise in a warm place for 20 minutes.

2 Meanwhile, preheat oven to 200C,400F, Gas 6. Melt the butter in a large frying pan, add the onions and cook gently for 10 minutes.

3 Divide the tomatoes and the onion mixture between the two pizza bases. Sprinkle each with basil or marjoram. Arrange cheeses on top and bake in oven for 25-30 minutes.

STILTON AND WATERCRESS TART

V

EASY!

A marvellous way to use up Stilton. Serve as a lunch or supper dish with salad.

Serves 4

Pastry
250g (8 oz) plain flour
pinch of salt
125g (4 oz) butter or margarine
about 3 tablespoons cold water

Filling
30g (1 oz) butter
2 bunches watercress, stalks removed
300g (10 oz) blue Stilton cheese, rind removed and diced
3 eggs
150 ml (5 fl oz) single cream
salt and pepper to taste
salad leaves and radishes to serve

1 Preheat oven to 200C,400F, Gas 6. To make pastry, sieve flour and salt into a large bowl. Rub in butter or margarine until the mixture resembles breadcrumbs. Add the water and mix to a firm dough.

2 Roll out pastry on a lightly floured surface and use to line an oiled 20 cm (8 inch) flan tin. Prick base and chill for 15 minutes, then bake blind in oven for 10-12 minutes. Lower oven temperature to 180C,350F, Gas 4.

3 Meanwhile, to prepare filling melt butter in a large frying pan, add the watercress and cook for 1-2 minutes, stirring constantly, until just wilted. Drain in sieve, pressing out excess liquid, then arrange in the pastry case.

Tuck the Stilton cubes into the watercress.

4 Beat together eggs and cream, season with salt and pepper and pour into the flan case. Bake for 30-35 minutes or until set. Serve warm or cold with salad leaves and radishes.

35 *HAM AND TURKEY NIÇOISE*

REALLY EASY!

A colourful salad of new potatoes, French beans, strips of turkey and ham, olives, tomatoes, spring onions and eggs tossed in a garlic and mustard dressing.

Serves 4

750g (1½ lb) small new potatoes
salt and pepper to taste
125g (4 oz) French beans, topped and tailed
125g (4 oz) cooked turkey, cut into strips
250g (8 oz) ham, cut into strips
8 black olives
125g (4 oz) cherry tomatoes, halved
4 spring onions, sliced diagonally
2 hard-boiled eggs, shelled and quartered

Dressing

75 ml (2½ fl oz) olive oil
2 tablespoons red wine vinegar
½ clove garlic, crushed
1 tablespoon wholegrain mustard
pinch of sugar

1 Cook potatoes in a saucepan of boiling salted water for 10-12 minutes until just cooked. Drain and allow to cool. Blanch beans in boiling water, then refresh in cold water and drain. Transfer potatoes and beans to a large serving bowl.

2 Add turkey, ham, olives, cherry tomatoes, spring onions and egg to the bowl.

3 To make dressing, stir all ingredients together with salt and pepper in a small bowl until combined. Pour over the salad and toss gently to mix.

INDEX

almond cakes 113
apricot and orange relish 61
apricot sherry trifle 102
asparagus and ham gratins 32
avocado and crispy bacon salad 33

bacon, preparing and cooking 10
bacon and avocado salad, crispy 33
bacon-wrapped sausages 66
bavarois, chestnut 106-7
beans with tomato 69
beef, roast fillet of 50-51
brandy butter, orange and 110
brandy cream 110
bread sauce 59
broccoli in ginger soy sauce 76
bruschetta 16-17
brussels sprouts, almond 70
buche de noel 118-19
buttercream 118-19

cabbage stir-fry, three 79
cakes 113-29
caramel squares 140-41
carrots with cashew nuts, spicy 73
carving turkeys 8
cauliflower and blue cheese gratin 74
cauliflower and cress soup 30
cauliflower with puffy cheese topping 77
cheese dishes
  cheese mixture 44-5
  cheesy brown rice pie 53
  mozzarella and egg salad 37
  stilton and watercress tart 156-7
  stilton grapes 20
  three cheese pizza 154-5
chestnut and cranberry soup 26
chestnut bavarois 106-7
chicken, preparing and cooking 5-9, 44-5
chocolate Christmas pudding cake 120-21
chocolate slice, crunchy 134
chocolate truffle cakes, raspberry 108-9
chocolate truffles 131
Christmas cakes 114-17, 126-7
Christmas cookies 139
Christmas puddings 98-101
Christmas tree biscuits 136-7
cointreau soufflé, iced 97
coleslaw 78, 89, 90
compote, fruit 104
cranberry sauce 60
crudités with garlic dip 14-15
Cumberland sauce 60

desserts 97-109
desserts, sauces for 110-11
dips
  garlic 14
  pesto 13
  red bean 21
dressings 81, 83
  basil 91
  cheese 35
  chilli 38
  curried coconut 148-9
  garlic 87
  garlic and basil 86
  garlic and mustard 158
  honey 95
  mayonnaise and yogurt 89
  mustard 88
  orange 94
  pine nut 93
  pineapple mint 90
  red wine vinegar 84
drinks 22-4
duck with orange sauce 48-9
Dundee cake 128

gammon joints, preparing and cooking 10
garlic toasts 16-17
ginger crunch 135
gingerbread cake 129
gravlax with oysters 31
gravy 45, 51, 58

ham
  and asparagus gratins 32
  honey-glazed 42-3
  melon and Parma ham 35
  and mushroom rolls 152
  pear and prosciutto salad 36
  and potato cakes 153
  and turkey Niçoise 158

icings 120-21
  glacé 124
  lemon 129
  royal 114-15

lamb, roast 52
leeks, crispy 71
leftover poultry 8-9
leftovers, dishes with 144-58
liqueur butter sauces 110-11

Madeira cake, cherry 125
melon and Parma ham 35
melon sorbet 105
mince pies 132-3
mozzarella and egg salad 37

orange and brandy butter 110
orange shortbread 138
oysters with gravlax 31

Parma ham and melon 35
parsnips baked in sour cream 75
pavlova 103
pear and prosciutto salad 36
pecan and liqueur butter sauce 111
pesto stuffing 46
pizza, three cheese 154-5
port and nut stuffing 50-51
potato cakes 153
potatoes, rosemary 68
prawns with creamy pesto 13
puddings, Christmas 98-101

quail's eggs 37

raspberry chocolate truffle cakes 108-9
ratatouille 72
redcurrant jelly sauce 52
relish, apricot and orange 61
rice and nut stuffing 40
roasting times 7
roquefort and almond soup 27

salads
  beetroot 81
  carrots and apples 82
  chick-pea and pepper 93
  crispy bacon and avocado 33
  crunchy mangetout 83
  fennel and red onion 84
  Greek potato 92
  ham and turkey Niçoise 158
  Italian bean 85
  lentil and mushroom 95
  mixed green 91
  mozzarella and egg 37
  mustard potato 88
  pear and prosciutto 36
  pineapple and kiwi fruit slaw 90
  roast pepper 86
  smoked trout and chilli 38
  tomato basil 87
  turkey and three rice 148-9
  vegetable slaw with pesto dressing 89
  watercress and orange 94
salmon terrine, striped 28-9
sandwiches, turkey and stilton 146
sauces
  brandy and liqueur 110-11
  bread 59
  cranberry 60
  Cumberland 60
  ginger and lime 62
  ginger soy 76
  mushroom 152
sausages, bacon-wrapped 66
sherry trifle, apricot 102
shortbread
  caramel squares 140-41
  orange 138
shortcake, fruit 142
smoked salmon parcels 34
smoked trout and chilli salad 38
sorbet, melon 105
soufflé, iced cointreau 97
soups
  cauliflower and cress 30
  chestnut and cranberry 26
  creamy turkey 145
  roquefort and almond 27
spinach tarts 18-19
starters 26-38
stilton and watercress tart 156-7
stilton grapes 20
stock, turkey 9
stollen 122-3
storing perishable foods 10-11
stuffing poultry 6
stuffings 44
  fig and pecan 65
  oaty stuffing balls 63
  pesto 46
  port and nut 50-51
  raisin, apple and ginger 64
  rice and nut 40-41

thawing times 5
trifle, apricot sherry 102
trout and chilli salad, smoked 38
trussing poultry 6
turkey
  and cheese muffins 147
  and chutney loaf 144
  creole 151
  dishes with leftovers 144-51, 158
  and ham Niçoise 158
  hash 150
  pesto stuffed turkey fillets 46-7
  preparing and cooking 5-9, 40-41
  soup 145
  and stilton open sandwiches 146
  and three rice salad 148-9

vegetarian recipes
  bruschetta 16-17
  cakes 113-29
  cheesy brown rice pie 53
  Christmas cakes 114-17, 126-7
  Christmas puddings 100-101
  crudités with garlic dip 14-15
  desserts 97, 100-105, 108-111
  mozzarella and egg salad 37
  ratatouille 72
  red bean dip 21
  salads 81-4, 86-95
  soups 26-7, 30
  spicy vegetable loaf 56
  spinach tarts 18-19
  stilton and watercress tart 156-7
  stilton grapes 20
  tea time snacks 131, 134-42
  three cheese pizza 154-5
  vegetable filo slice 54-5
  vegetables 68-79